GOLDEN AGE HEROES TO INK AND DRAW! GUIDEBOOK

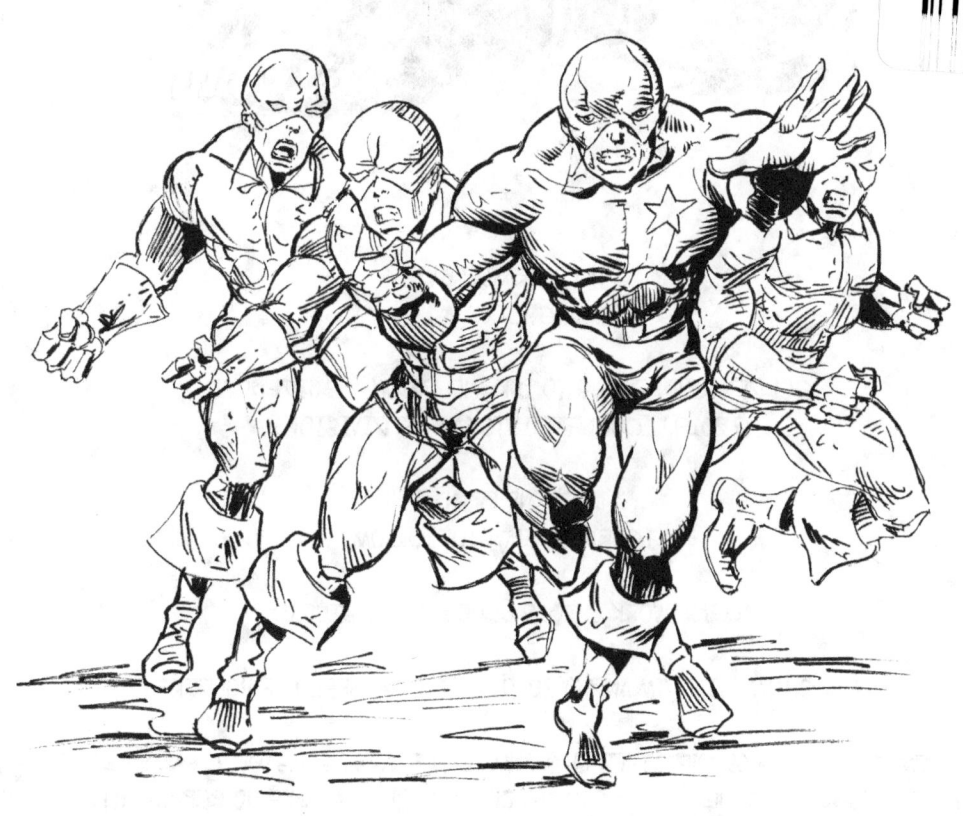

AN INKING & DRAWING

COLLECTION OF PUBLIC DOMAIN

CHARACTERS

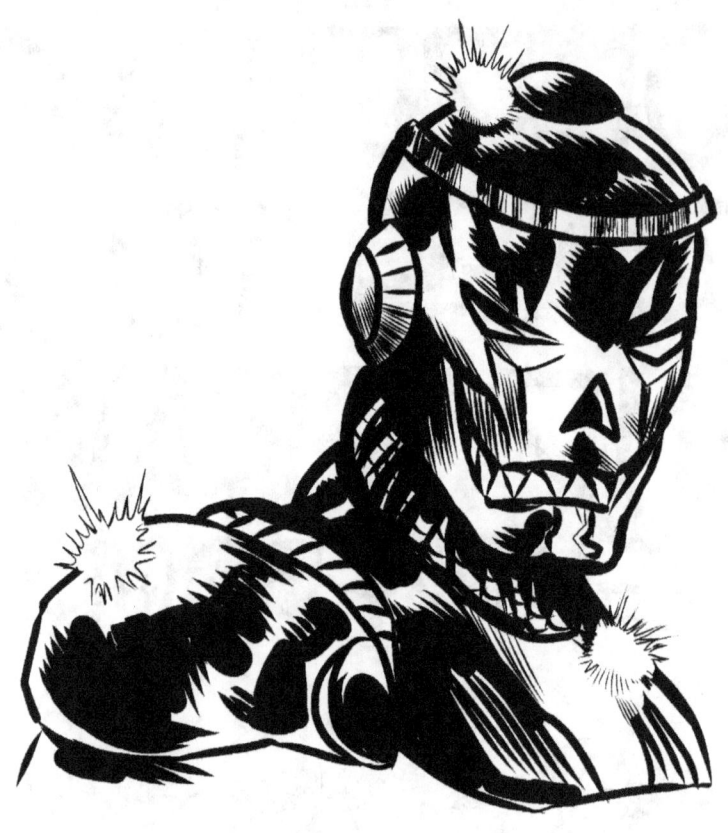

ILLUSTRATED BY
A. G. CEGLIA

GOLDEN AGE HEROES TO INK AND DRAW! - GUIDEBOOK
© 2019 LICORNE PRINTS (A BMS DIVISION).

LICORNE PRINTS
LICORNE@BEMYSTUDIO.COM

ALL ARTWORK © 2019 BLUE MONKEY STUDIO.

ALL CHARACTERS TM AND © 2019 OF THEIR RESPECTIVE HOLDERS

THIS IS AN ACADEMIC WORK. THESE AND OTHER ©, ® AND TM APPEARS AS HISTORIC EXAMPLES FOR SCHOLARLY PURPOSES. ALL RIGHTS RESERVED. BLUE MONKEY STUDIO OR DODO PRINTS MAKE NO REPRESENTATION OF ANY RIGHTS TO SAID ©, ® AND TM.

ANY OMMISSION OR INCORRECT INFORMATION SHOULD BE TRANSMITTED TO THE AUTHOR OR THE PUBLISHER SO IT CAN BE RECTIFIED IN FUTURE EDITION OF THIS BOOK.

NO PART OF THIS BOOK MAY BE USED OR REPRODUCED IN ANY MANNER WHATSOEVER WITHOUT WRITTEN PERMISSION EXCEPT IN THE CASE OF BRIEF QUOTATIONS EMBODIED IN CRITICAL ARTICLES AND REVIEWS.

CHARACTER LIST

ALIAS THE DRAGON
(HARRY "A" CHESLER, SKYROCKET COMICS –ONE SHOT, 1944)

ATOMIC THUNDERBOLT
(REGOR COMPANY, ATOMIC THUNDERBOLT #1, FEB. 1946)

BARRY KUDA & ALGIE
(HARRY "A" CHESLER, YANKEE COMICS #2, NOV. 1941)

BLACK DWARF
(HARRY "A" CHESLER, SPOTLIGHT COMICS #1, NOV. 1944)

BLACK SATAN
(HARRY "A" CHESLER, YANKEE COMICS #1, SEPT. 1941)

BLACK TERROR
(BETTER/NEDOR/STANDARD, EXCITING COMICS #9, MAY 1941)

CAPTAIN BATTLE & KANE
(HARRY "A" CHESLER, CAPTAIN BATTLE COMICS #3, WINTER 1942)

CAPTAIN GLORY
(HARRY "A" CHESLER, PUNCH COMICS #1, DEC. 1941)

DR. FROST
(PRIZE, PRIZE COMICS #7, DEC. 1940)

DR. VAMPIRE
(HARRY "A" CHESLER, SKYROCKET COMICS #1, 1944)

DYNAMIC BOY, DYNAMIC MAN'S SIDEKICK
(HARRY "A" CHESLER, DYNAMIC COMICS #11, SEPT. 1944)

DYNAMIC MAN
(HARRY "A" CHESLER, DYNAMIC COMICS #1, OCT. 1941)

ECHO
(HARRY "A" CHESLER, YANKEE COMICS #1, SEPT. 1941)

ENCHANTED DAGGER
(HARRY "A" CHESLER, YANKEE COMICS #1, SEPT. 1941)

FIGHTING YANK
(BETTER/NEDOR/STANDARD, STARTLING COMICS #10, SEPT. 1941)

FIREBRAND
(HARRY "A" CHESLER, YANKEE COMICS #1, SEPT. 1941)

FOUR COMRADES
(BETTER/NEDOR/STANDARD, STARTLING COMICS #16, AUG. 1942)

GREEN KNIGHT & LANCE
(HARRY "A" CHESLER, DYNAMIC COMICS #2, DEC. 1941)

HALE THE MAGICIAN
(HARRY "A" CHESLER, DYNAMIC COMICS #1, SEPT. 1941)

JOHNNY REBEL
(HARRY "A" CHESLER, YANKEE COMICS #2, NOV. 1941)

JUDY OF THE JUNGLE
(BETTER/NEDOR/STANDARD, EXCITING COMICS #55, MAY 1947)

KAZA
(AJAX-FARRELL, FANTASTIC FEARS #8, JUL.-AUG. 1954)

KITTY KELLY
(HARRY "A" CHESLER, PUNCH COMICS #1, DEC. 1941)

LADY SATAN
(HARRY "A" CHESLER, DYNAMIC COMICS #2, DEC. 1941)

MASTER KEY
(HARRY "A" CHESLER, SCOOP COMICS #1, NOV. 1941)

MEKANO
(BETTER/NEDOR/STANDARD, WONDER COMICS #1, MAY 1944)

MR. E
(HARRY "A" CHESLER, PUNCH COMICS #1, DEC. 1941)

MISS MASQUE
(BETTER/NEDOR/STANDARD, EXCITING COMICS #51, SEPT. 1946)

MOTHER HUBBARD
(HARRY "A" CHESLER, SCOOP COMICS #1, NOV. 1941)

PHANTOM DETECTIVE
(BETTER/NEDOR/STANDARD, THRILLING COMICS #53, APR. 1946)

QUEEN MERMA, BARRY KUDA'S GIRLFRIEND
(HARRY "A" CHESLER, YANKEE COMICS #2, NOV. 1941)

ROCKET BOY
(HARRY "A" CHESLER, SCOOP COMICS #2, JAN. 1942)

ROCKETMAN & ROCKETGIRL
(HARRY "A" CHESLER, SCOOP COMICS #1, NOV. 1941)

SPIDER WOMAN
(HARRY "A" CHESLER, MAJOR VICTORY COMICS #1, 1944)

VEILED AVENGER
(HARRY "A" CHESLER, SPOTLIGHT COMICS #1, NOV. 1944)

YANKEE DOODLE JONES & DANDY
(HARRY "A" CHESLER, YANKEE COMICS #1, SEPT. 1941)

YANKEE BOY
(HARRY "A" CHESLER, YANKEE COMICS #2, NOV. 1941)

YANKEE GIRL
(HARRY "A" CHESLER, DYNAMIC COMICS #23, 1947)

HEROES INKING!

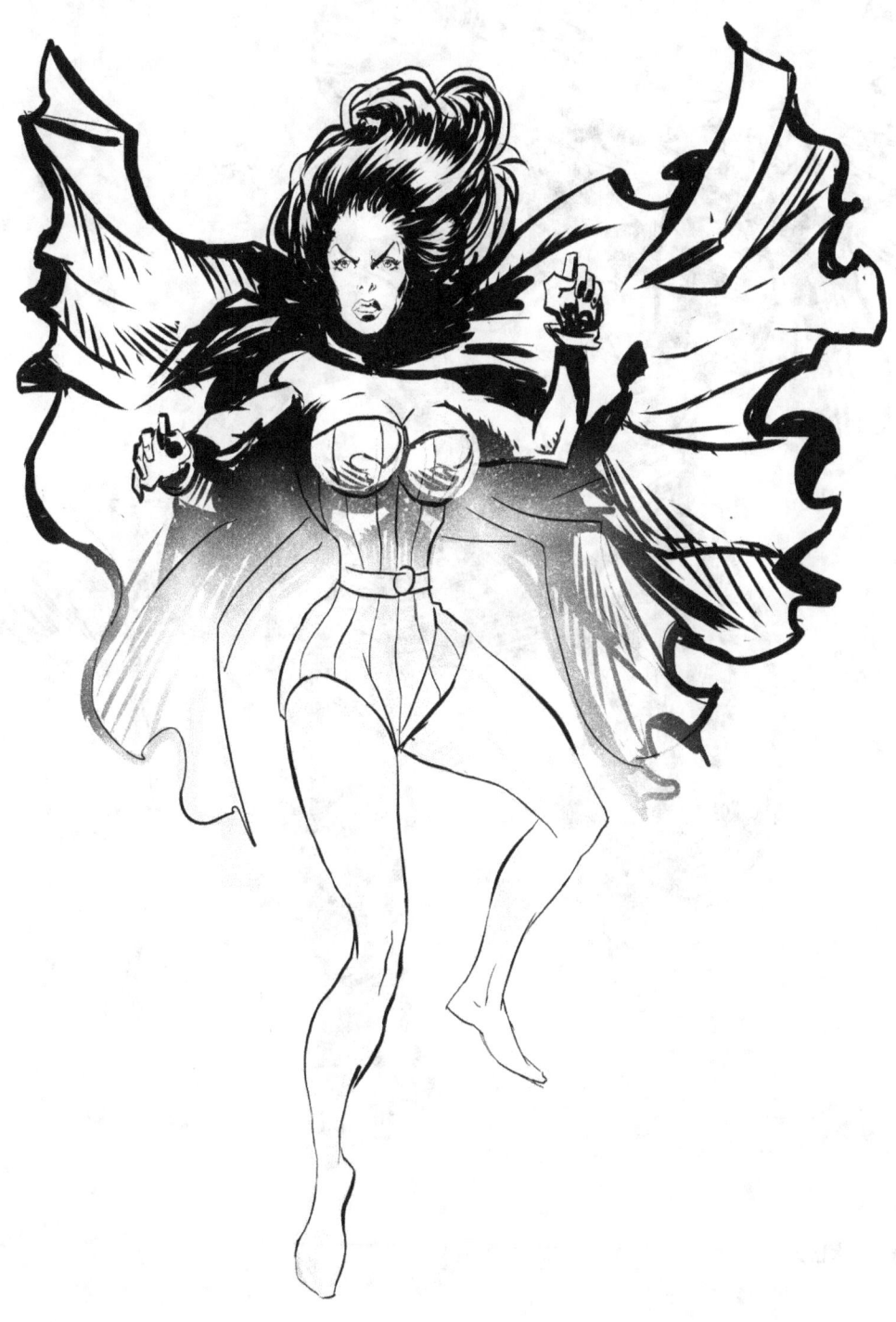

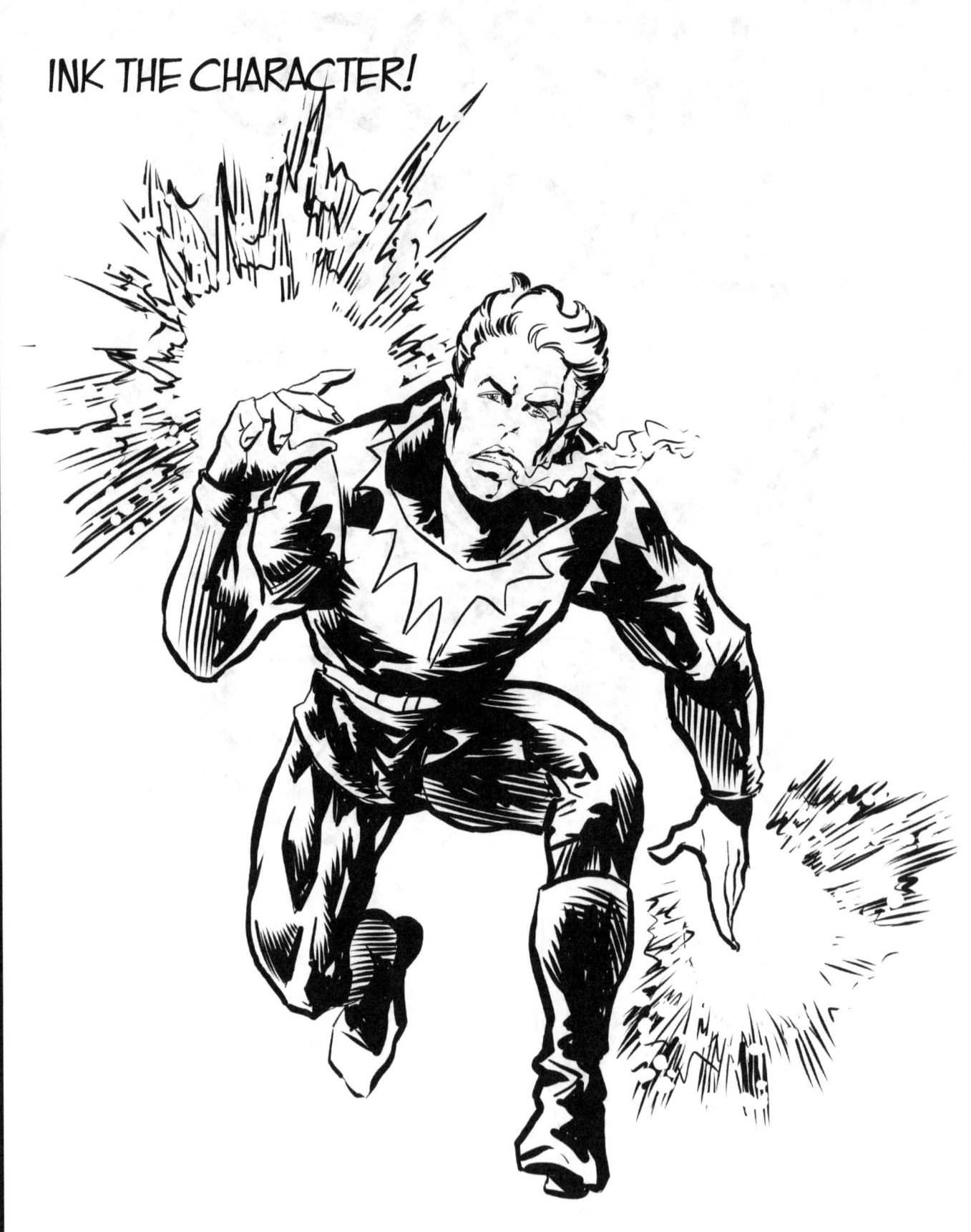

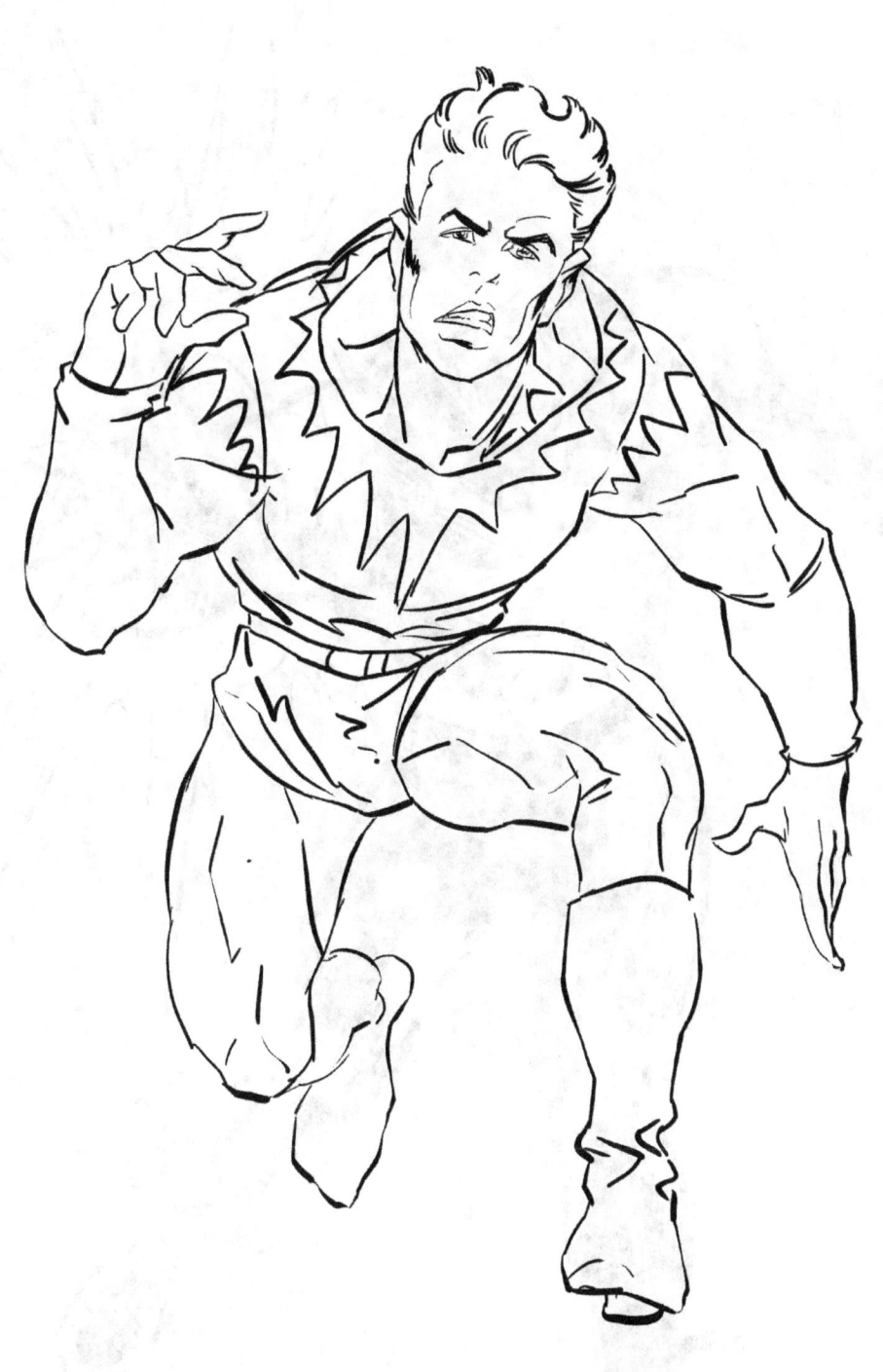

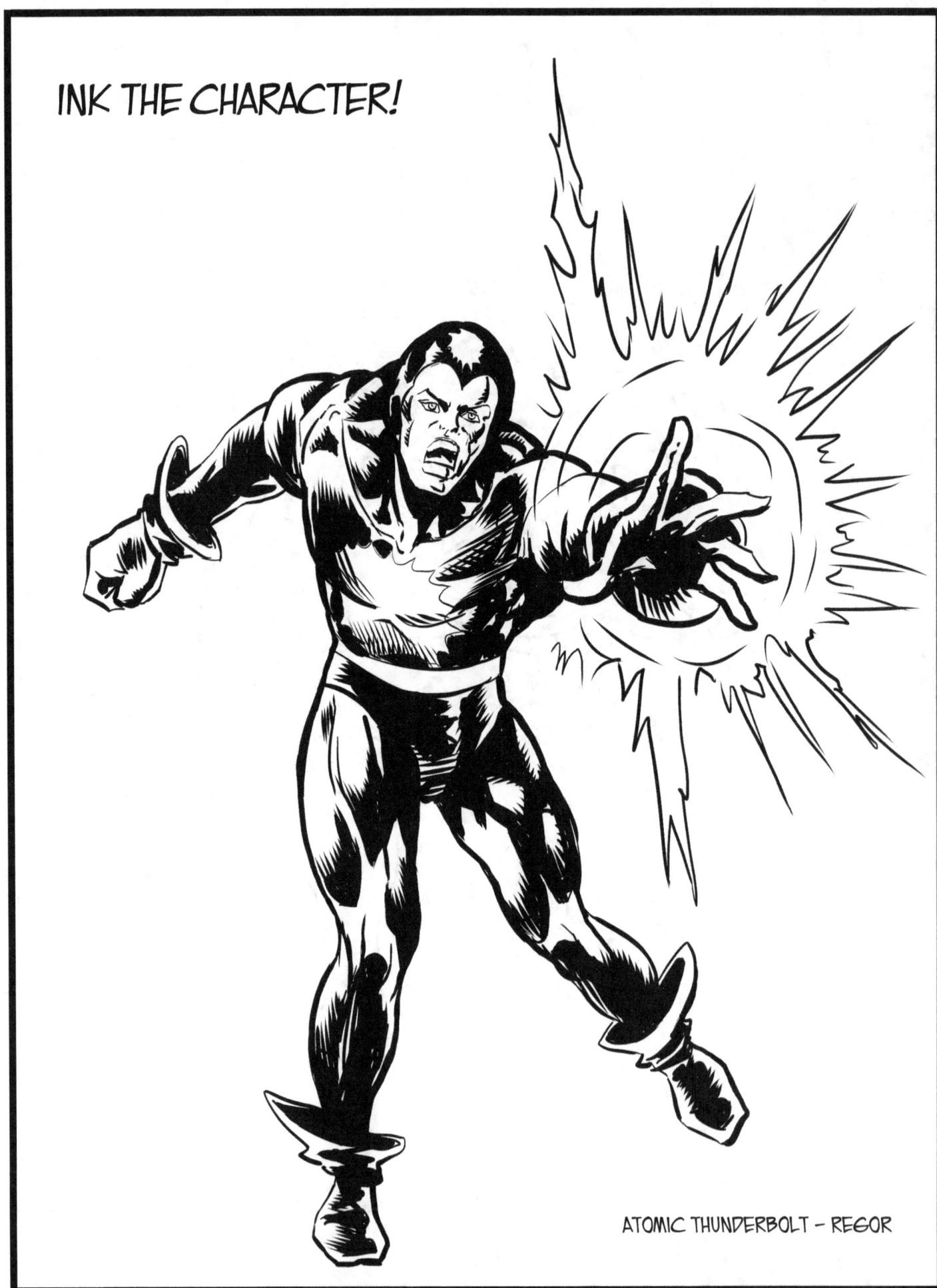

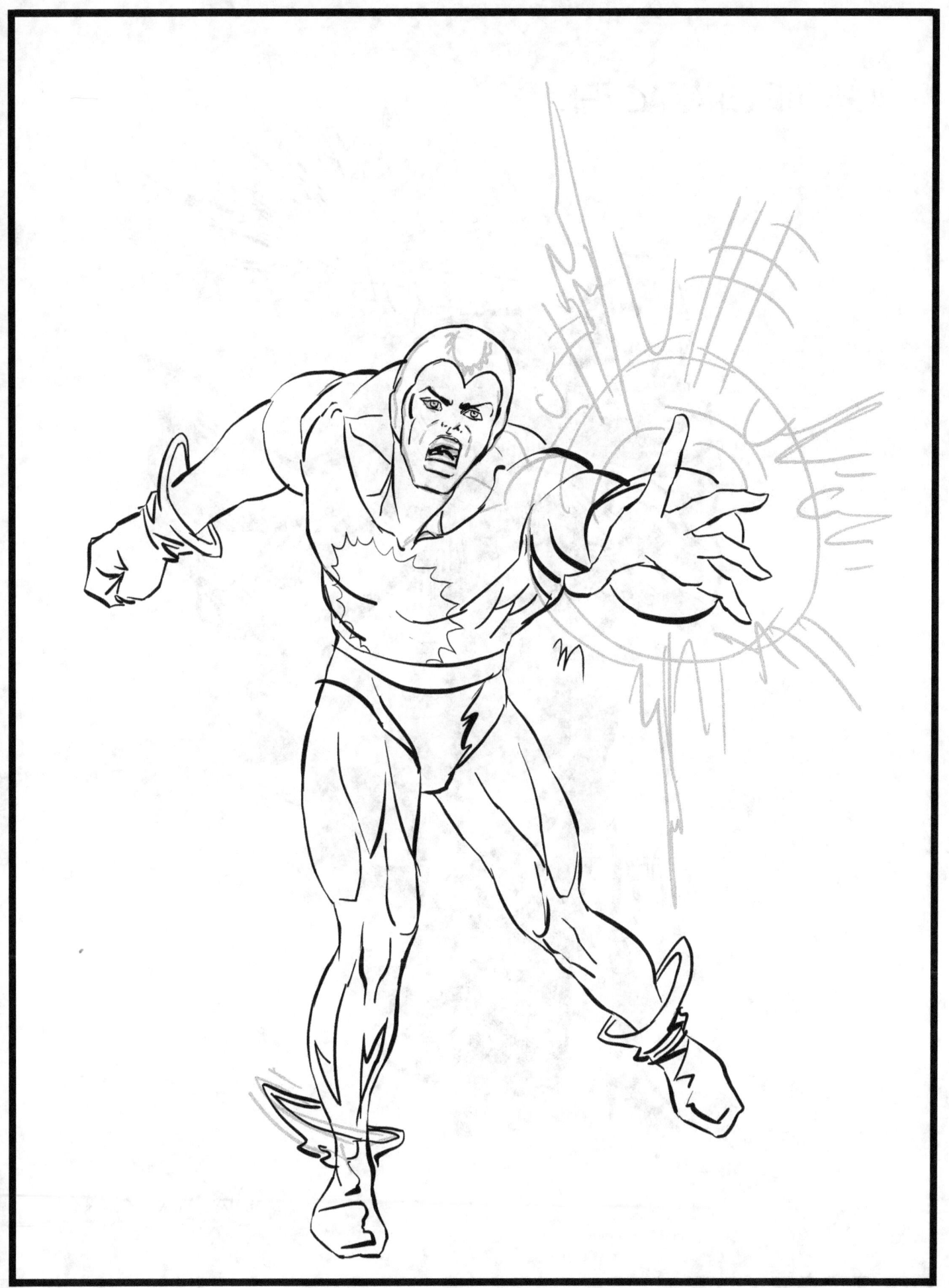

INK THE CHARACTER!

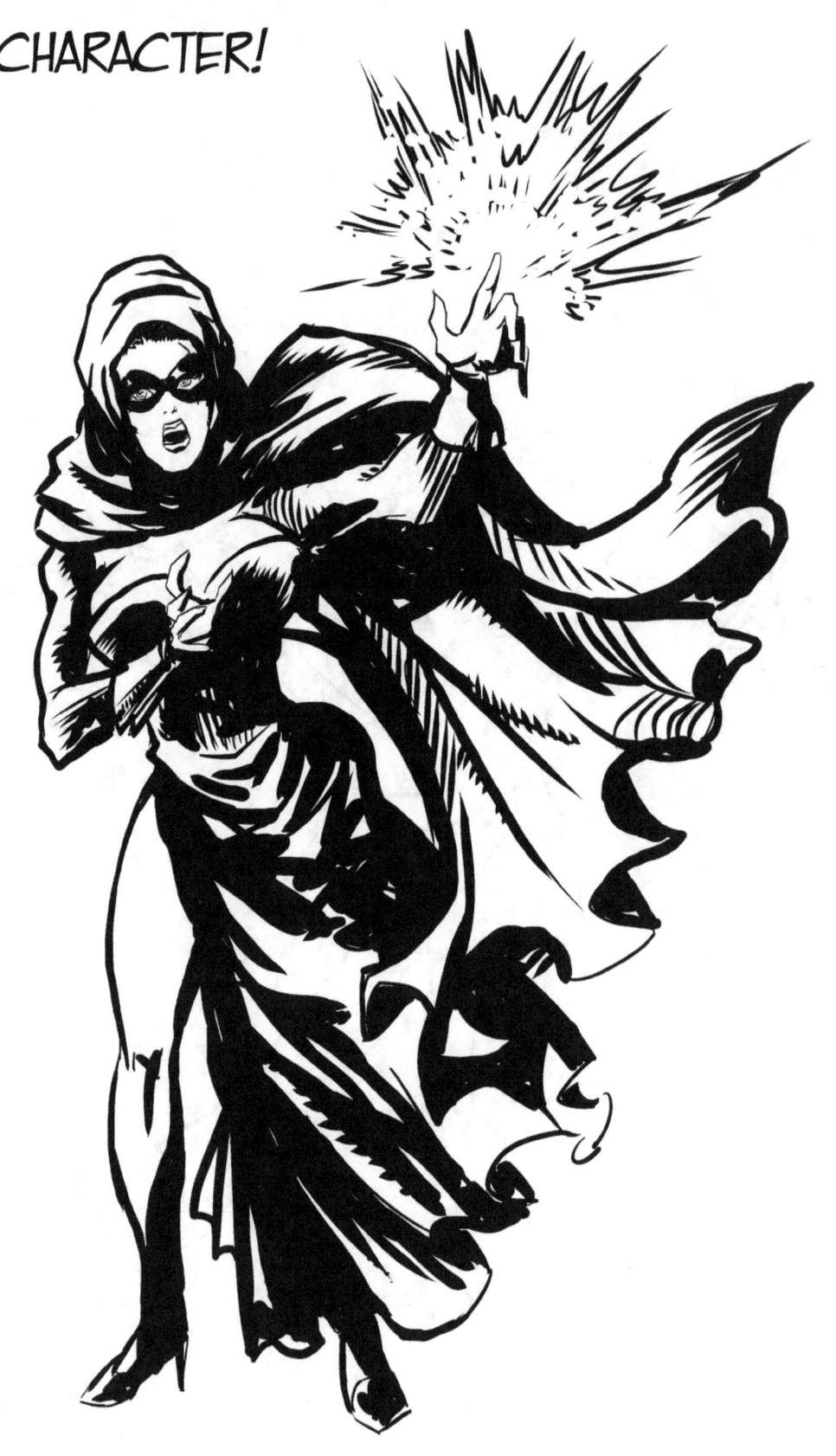

LADY SATAN - CHESLER

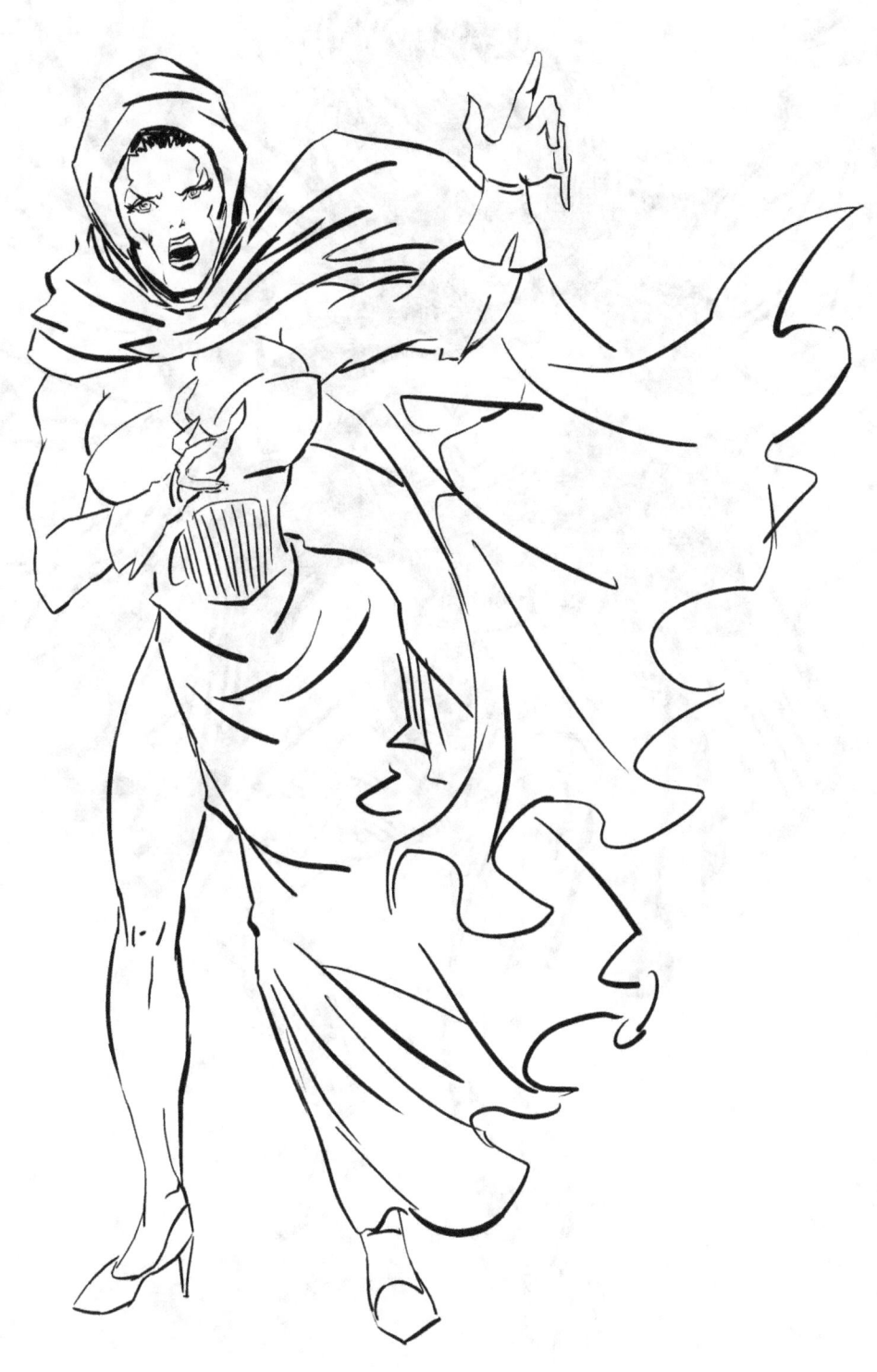

INK THE CHARACTER!

YANKEE GIRL – CHESLER

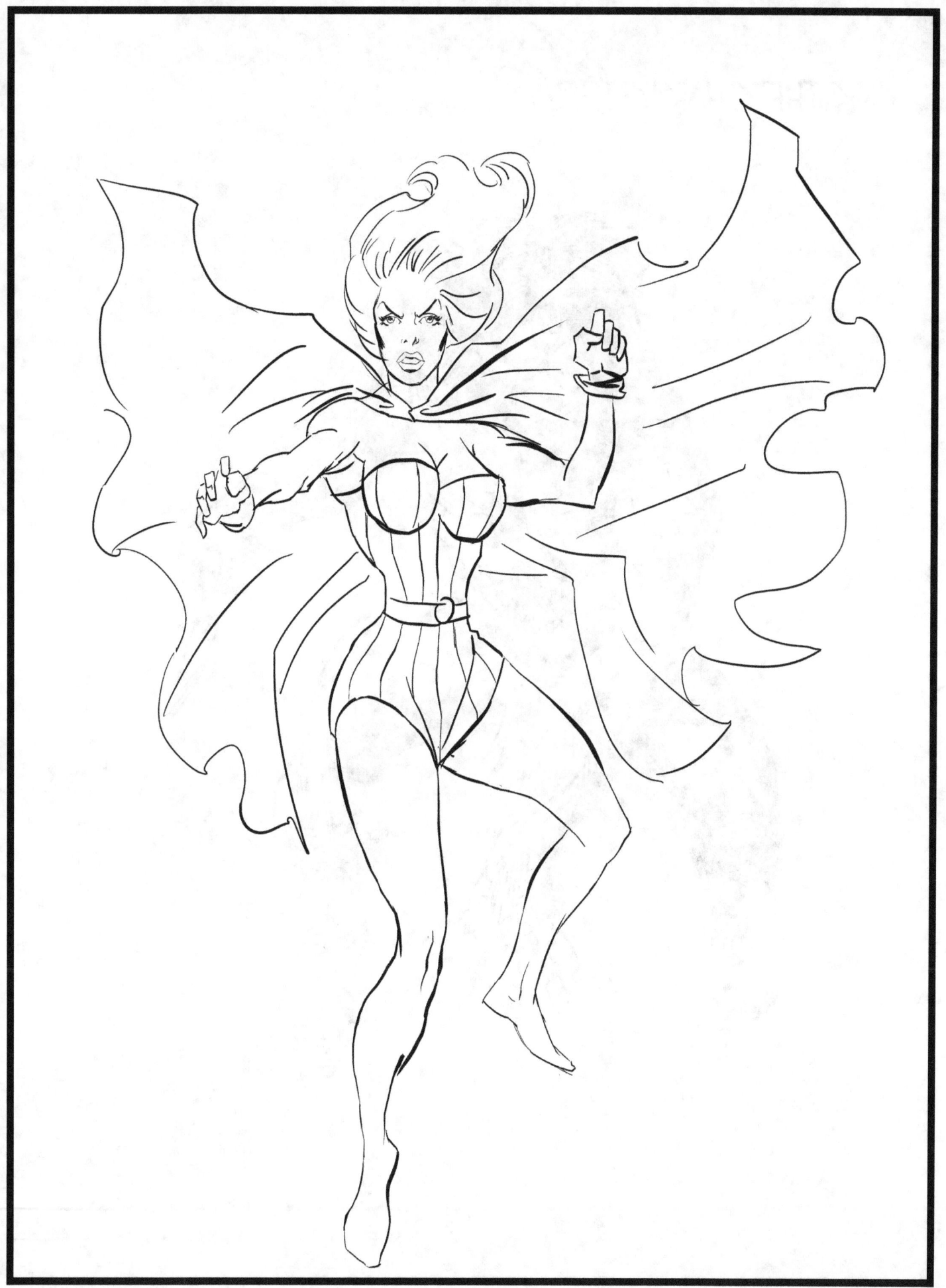

INK THE CHARACTER!

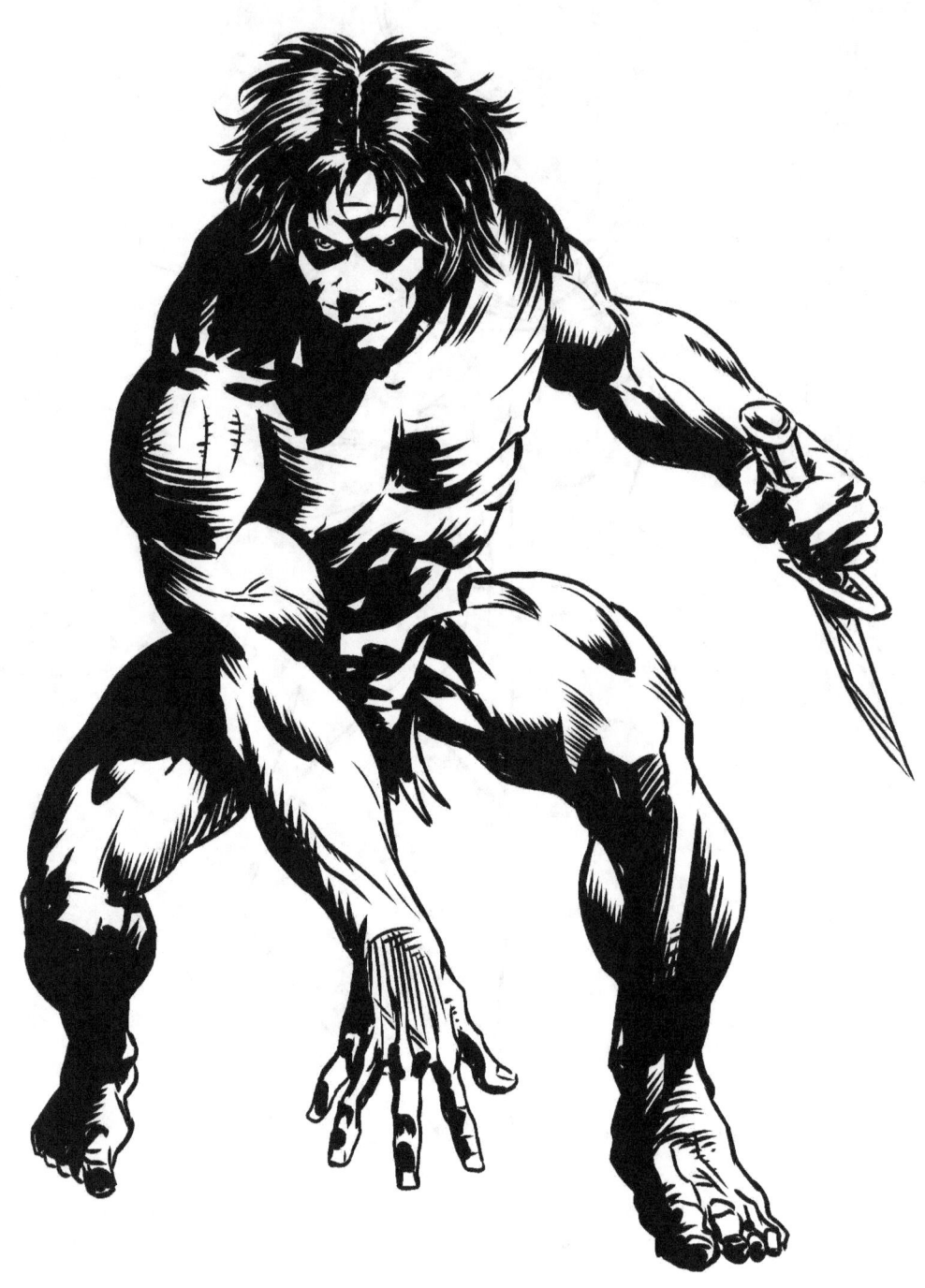

KAZA – AJAX-FARRELL

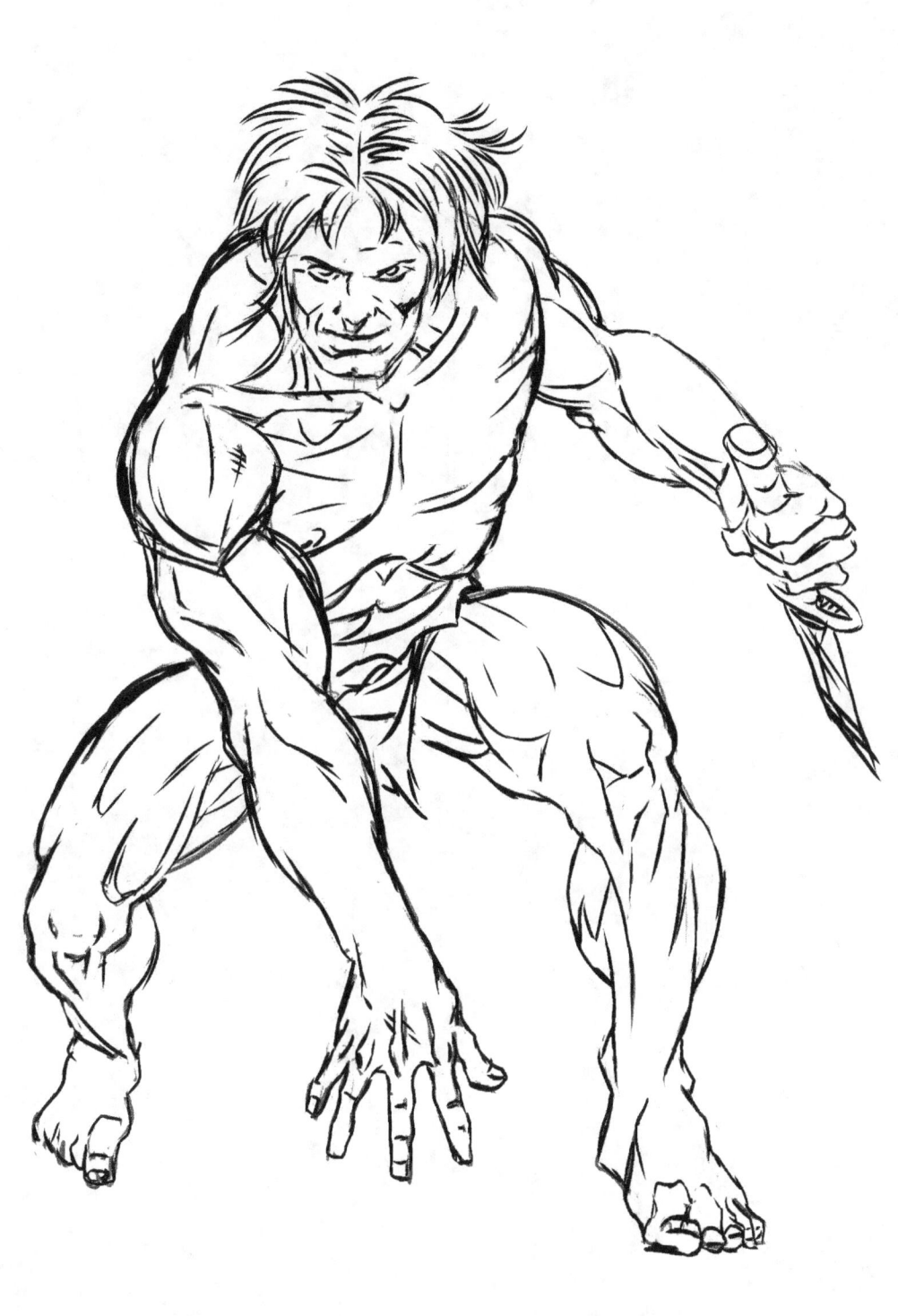

HEROES DRAWING!

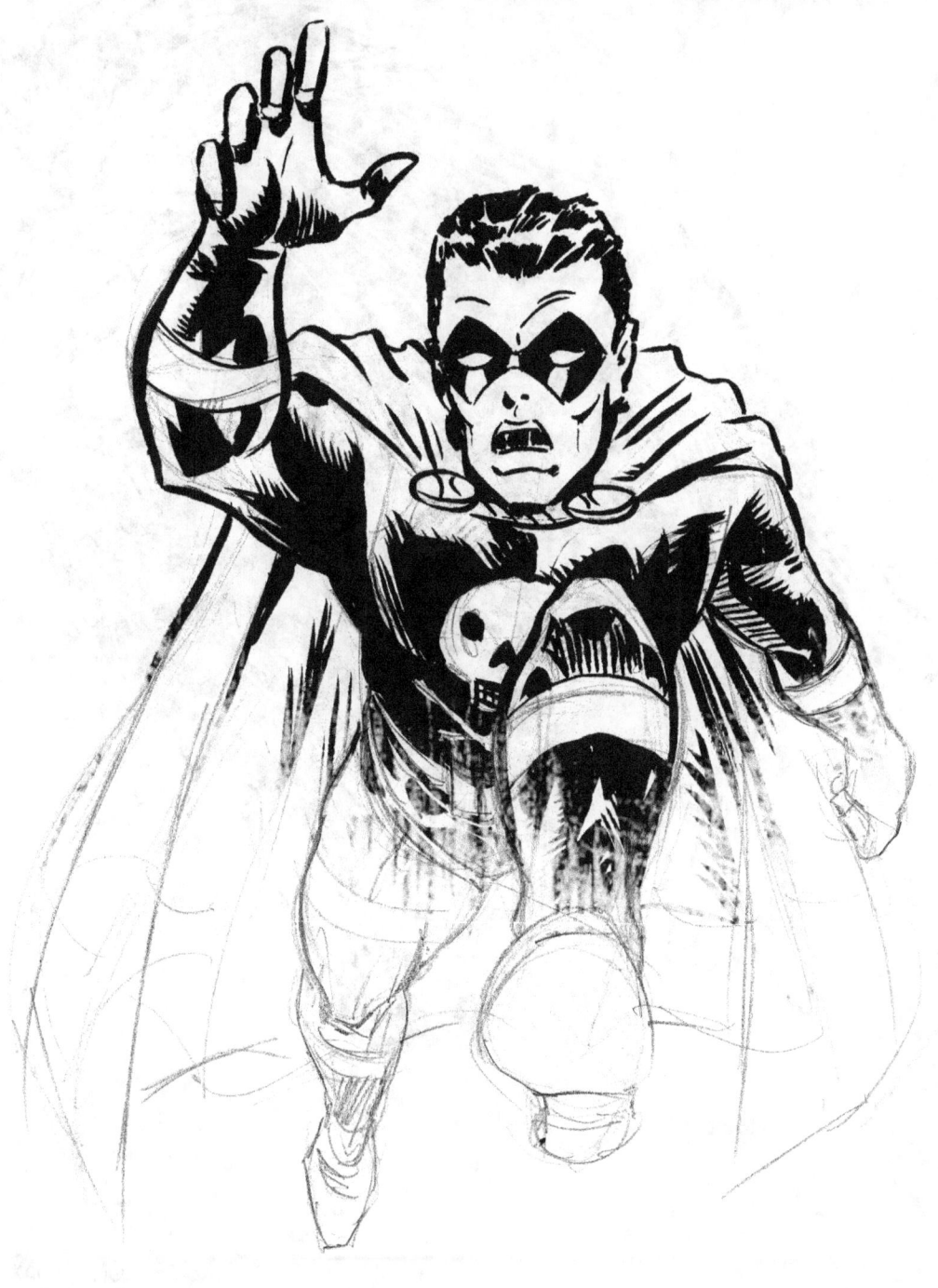

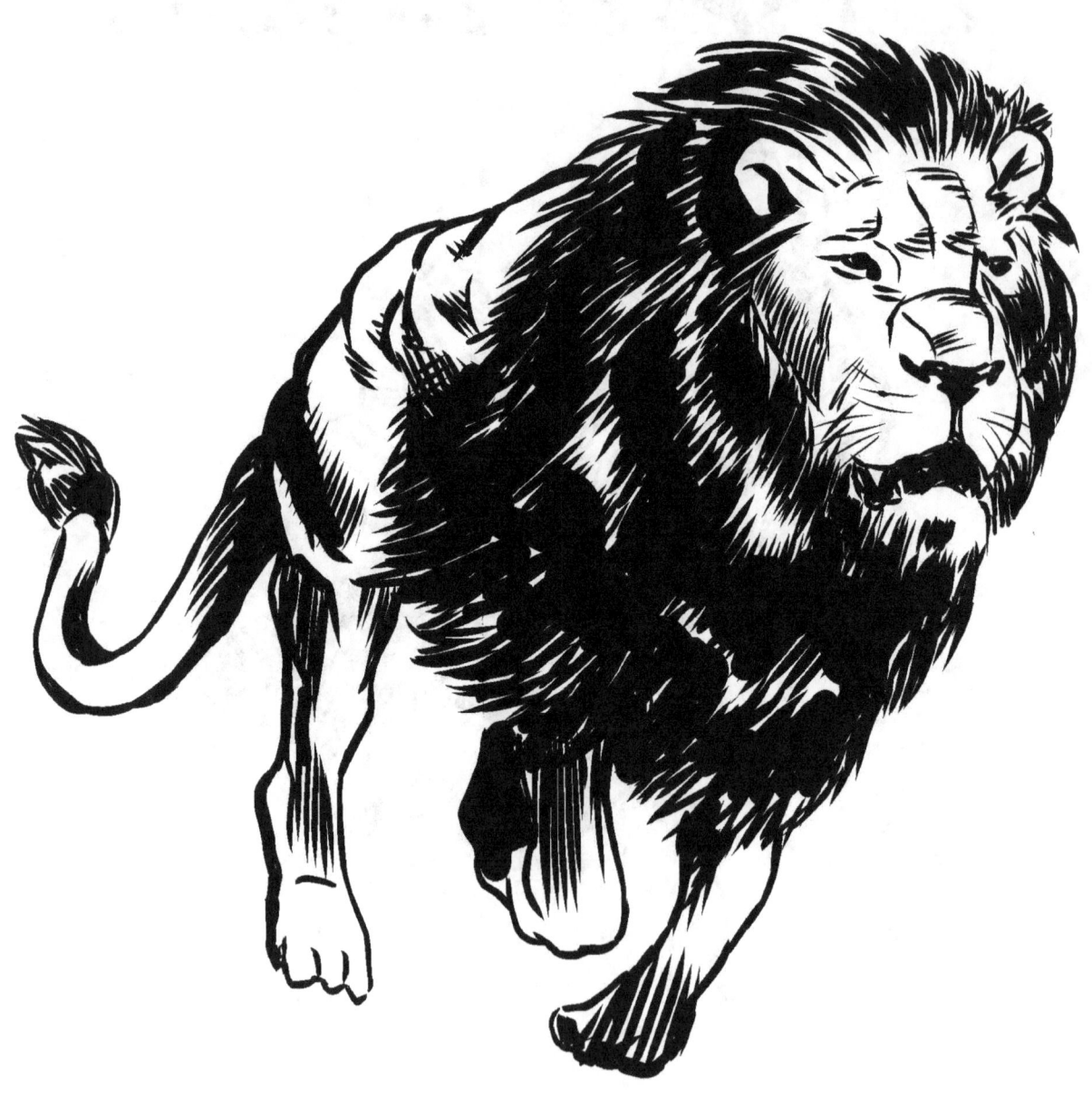

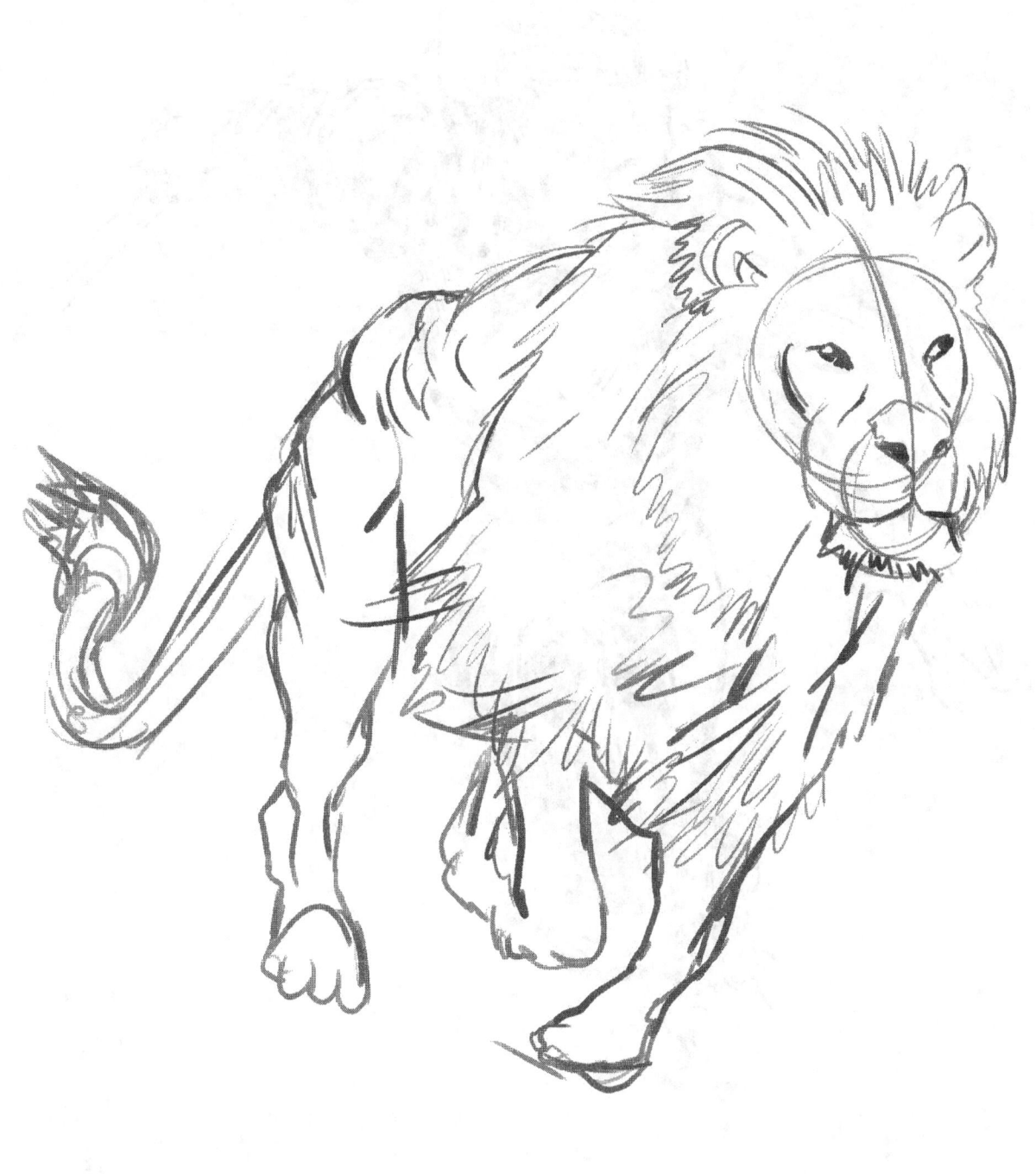

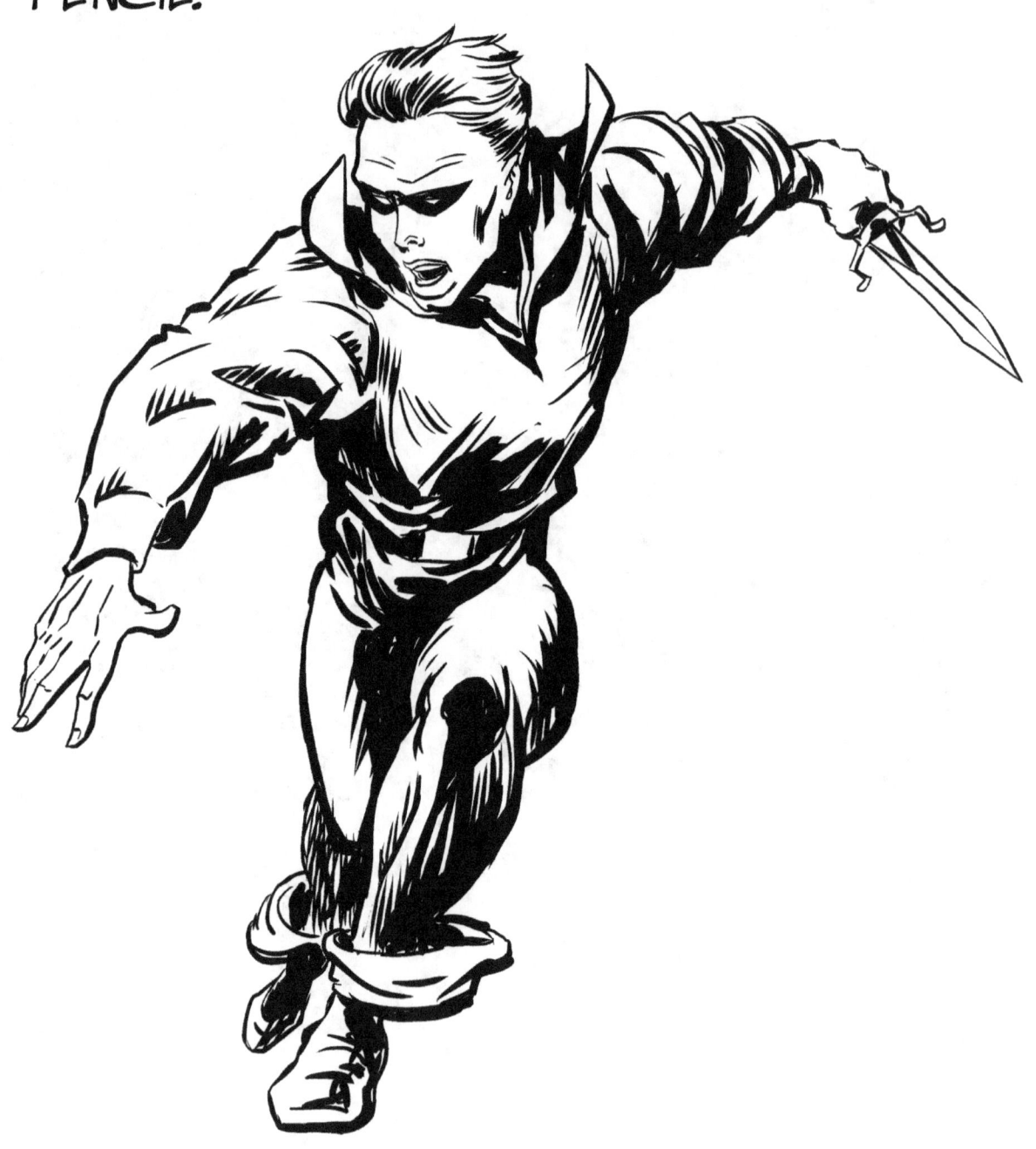

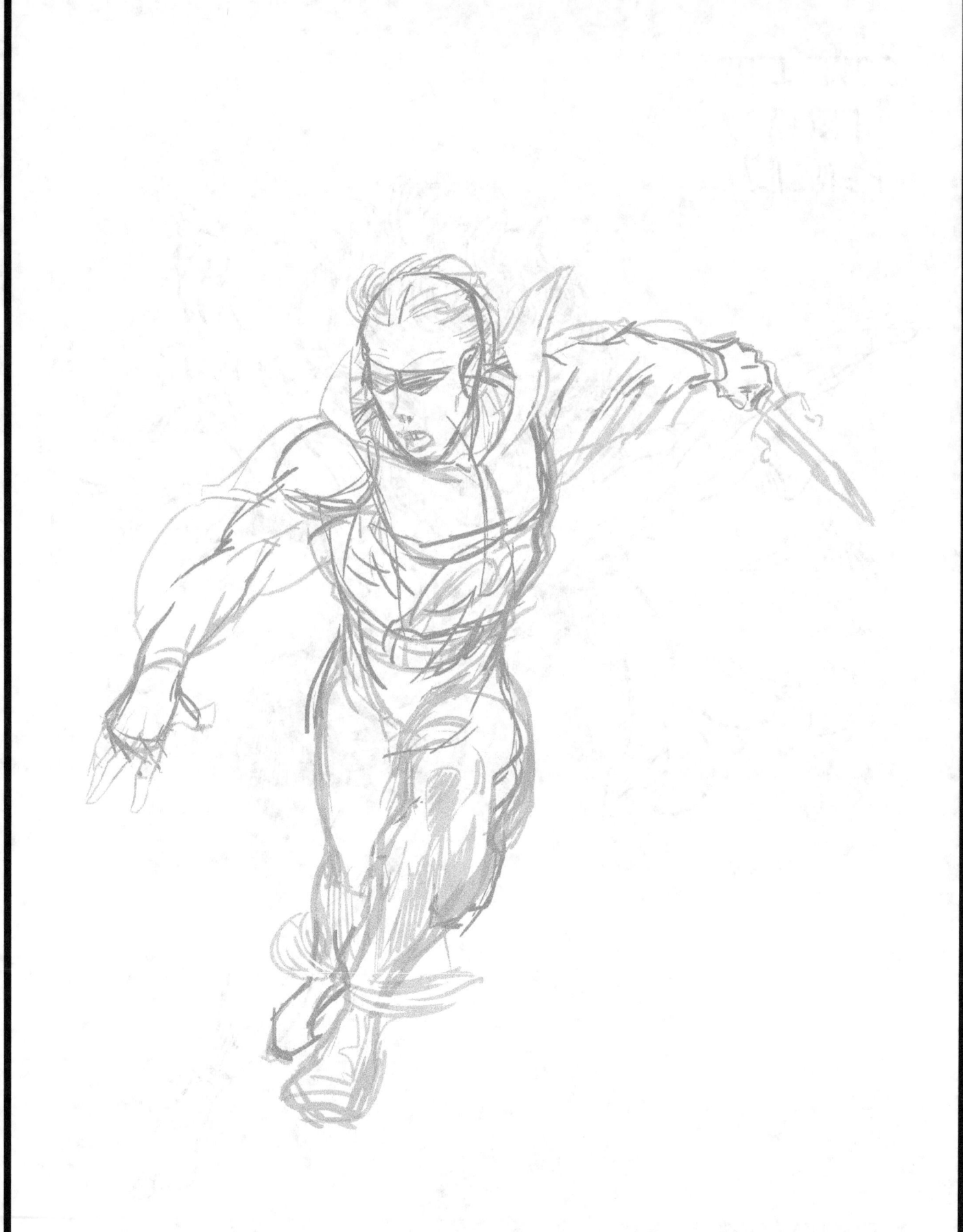

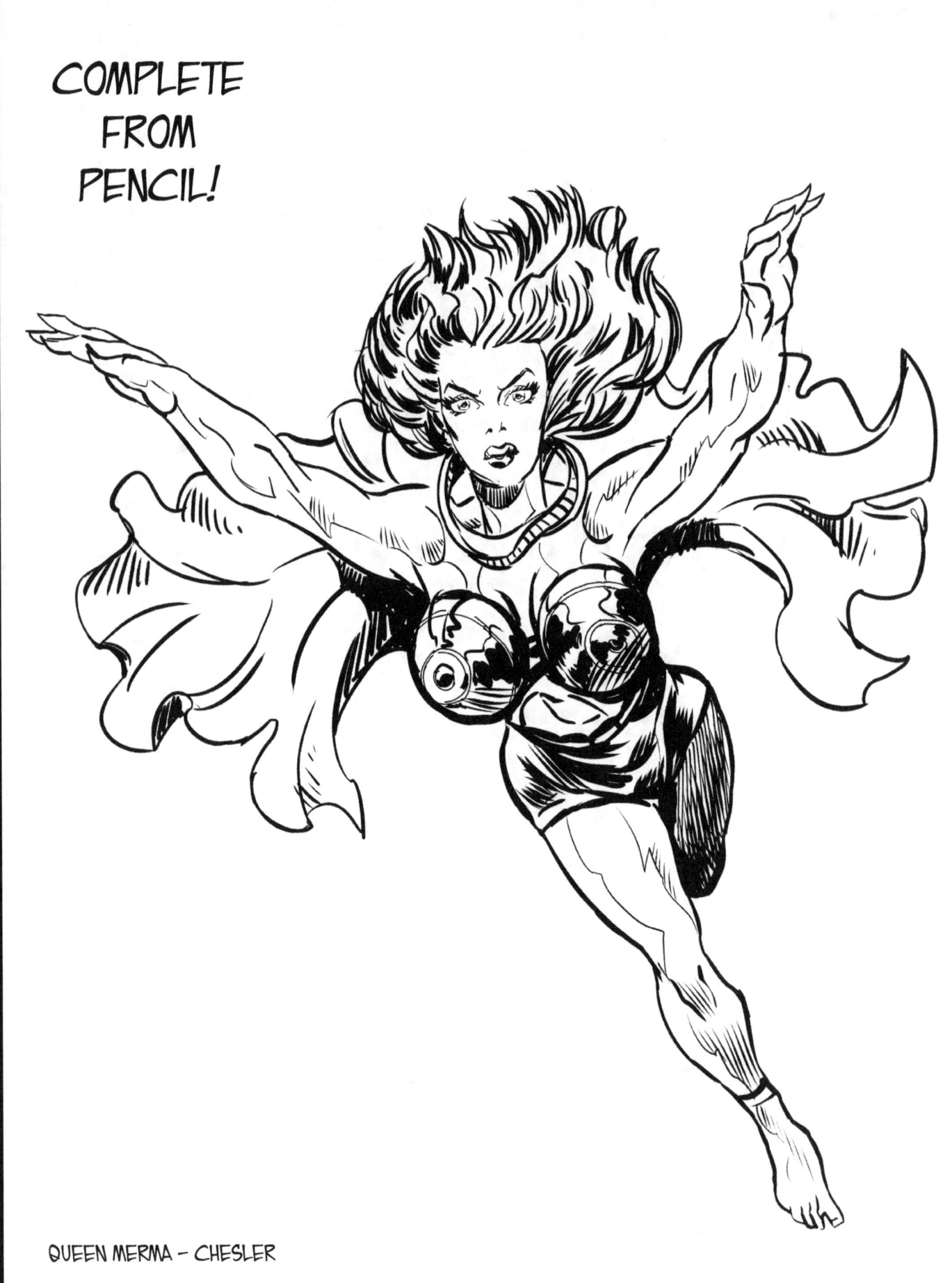

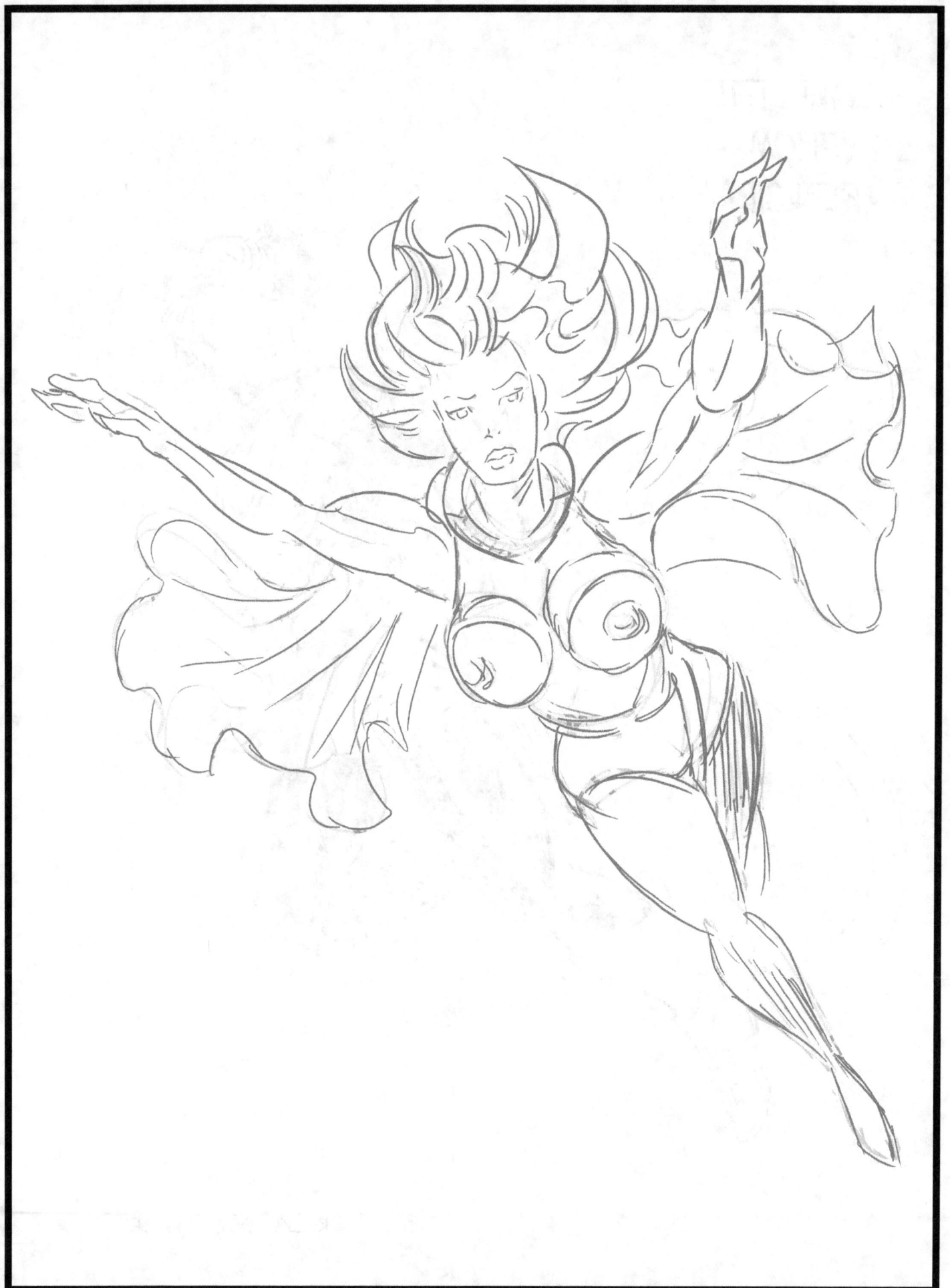

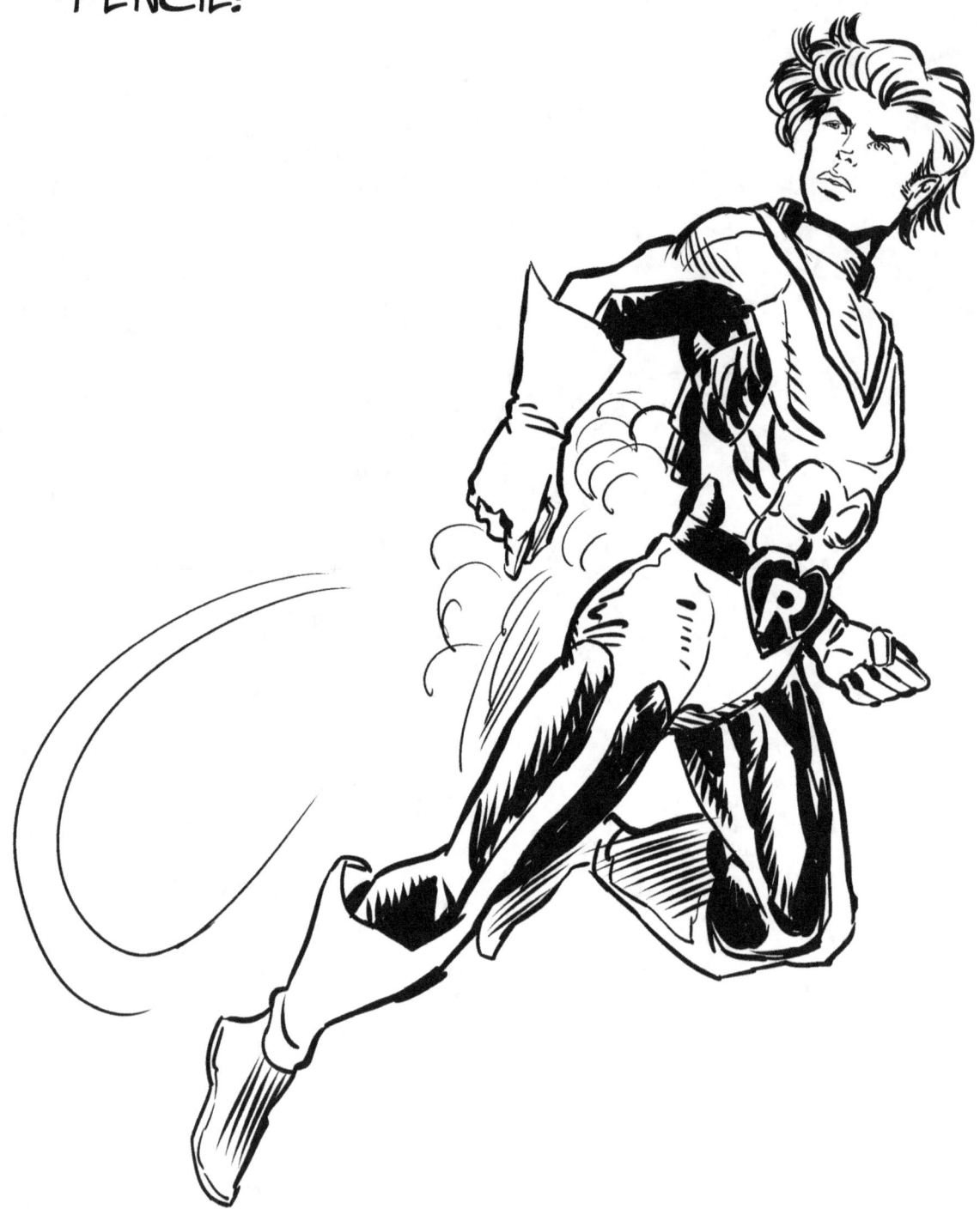

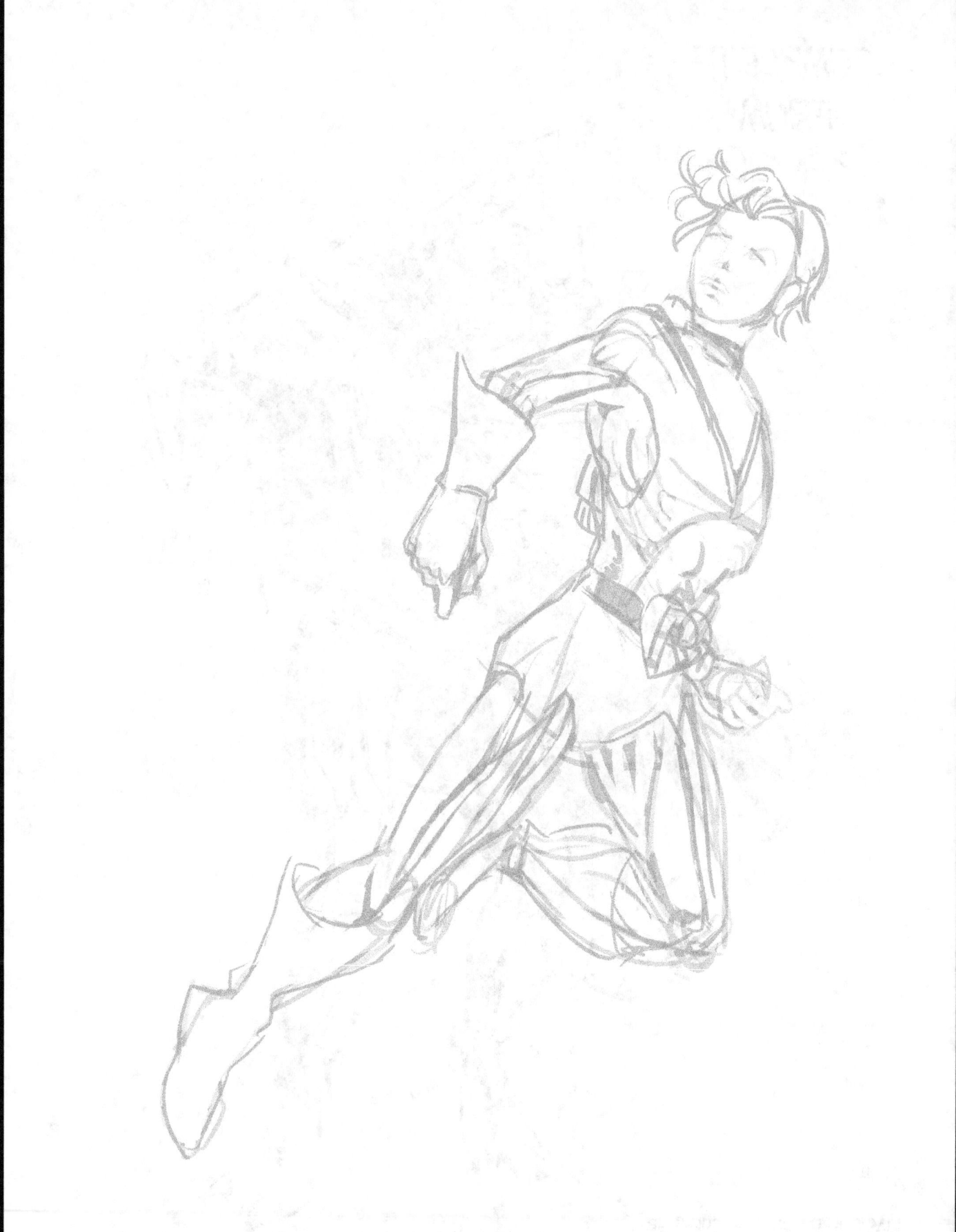

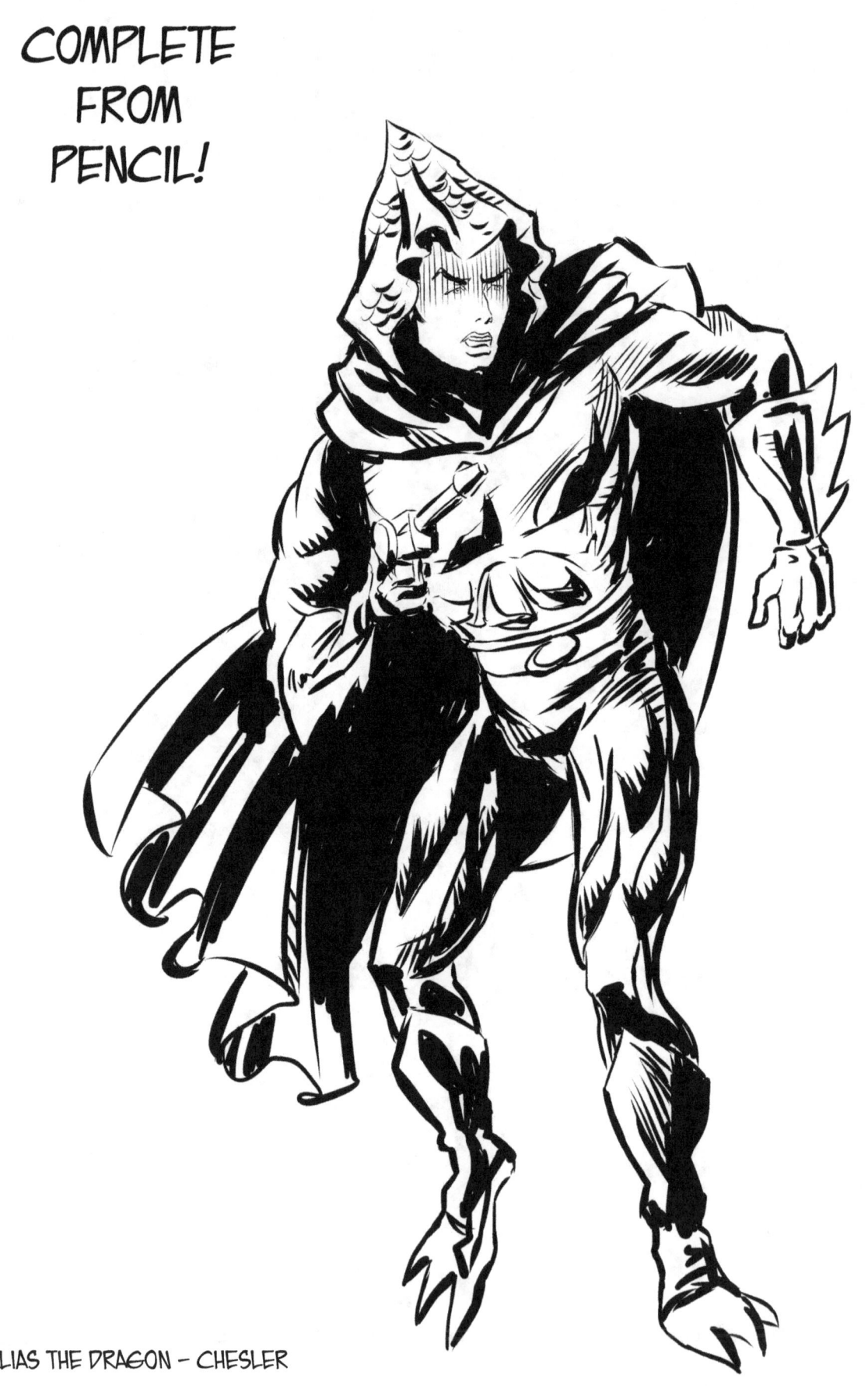

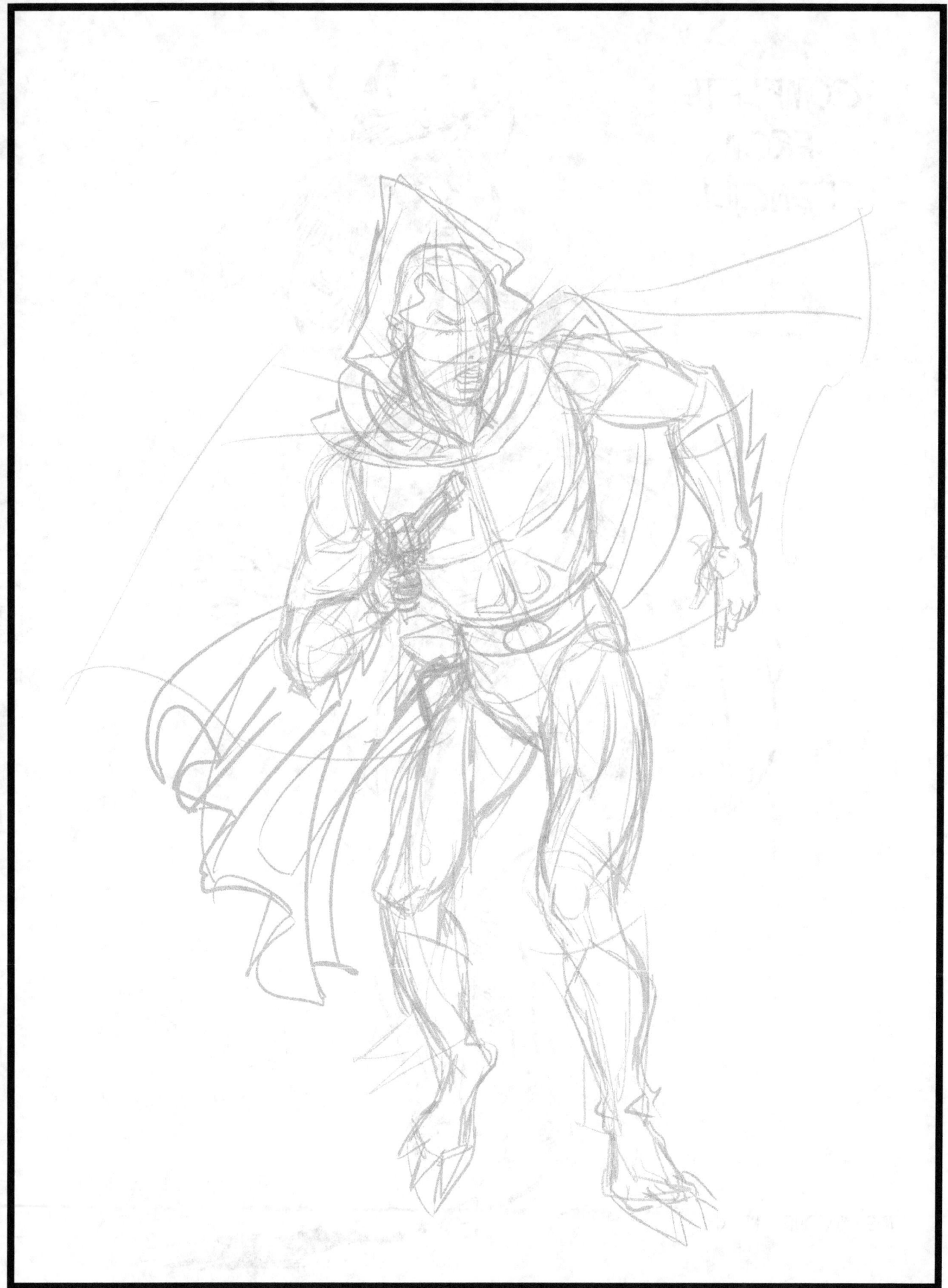

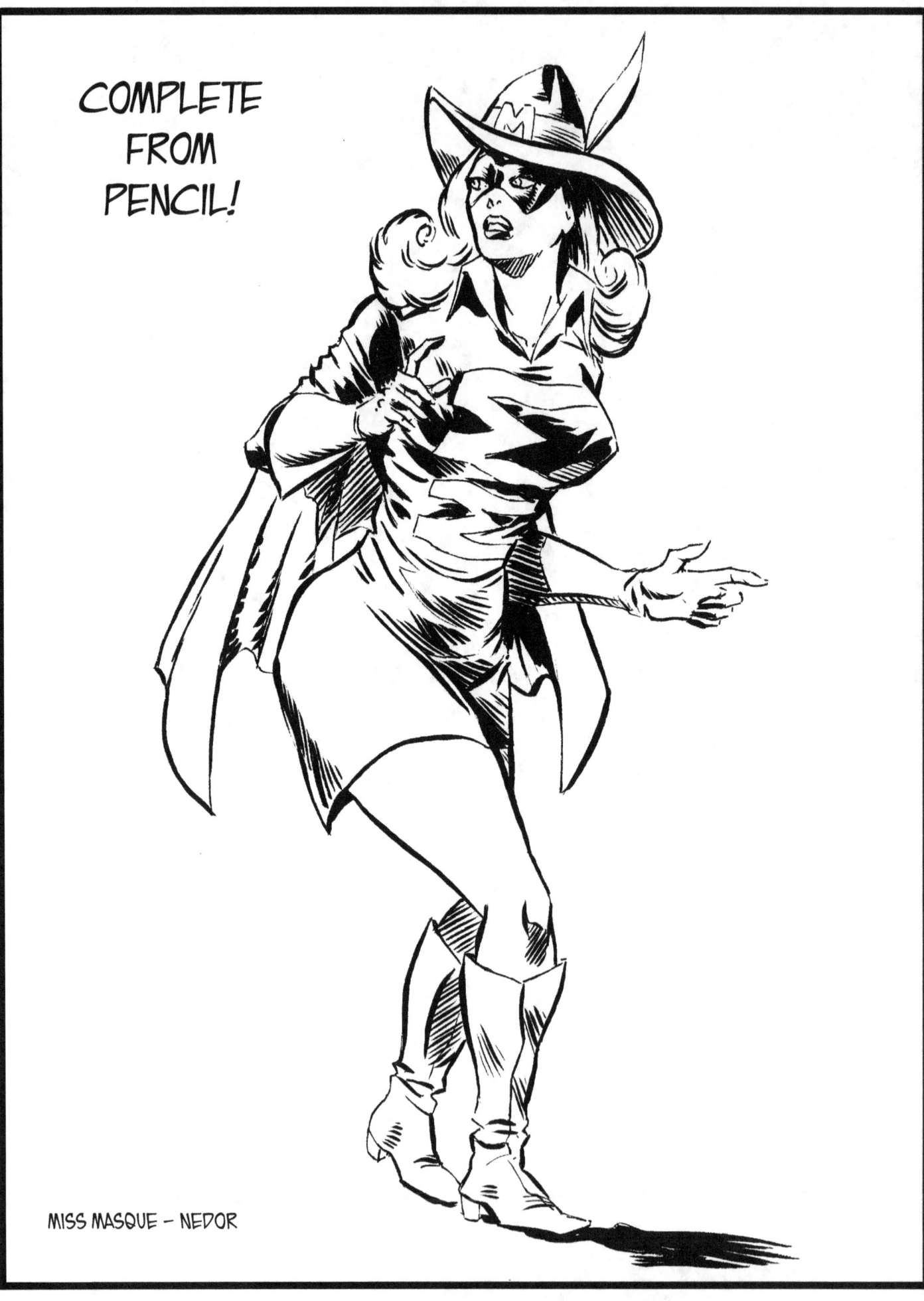

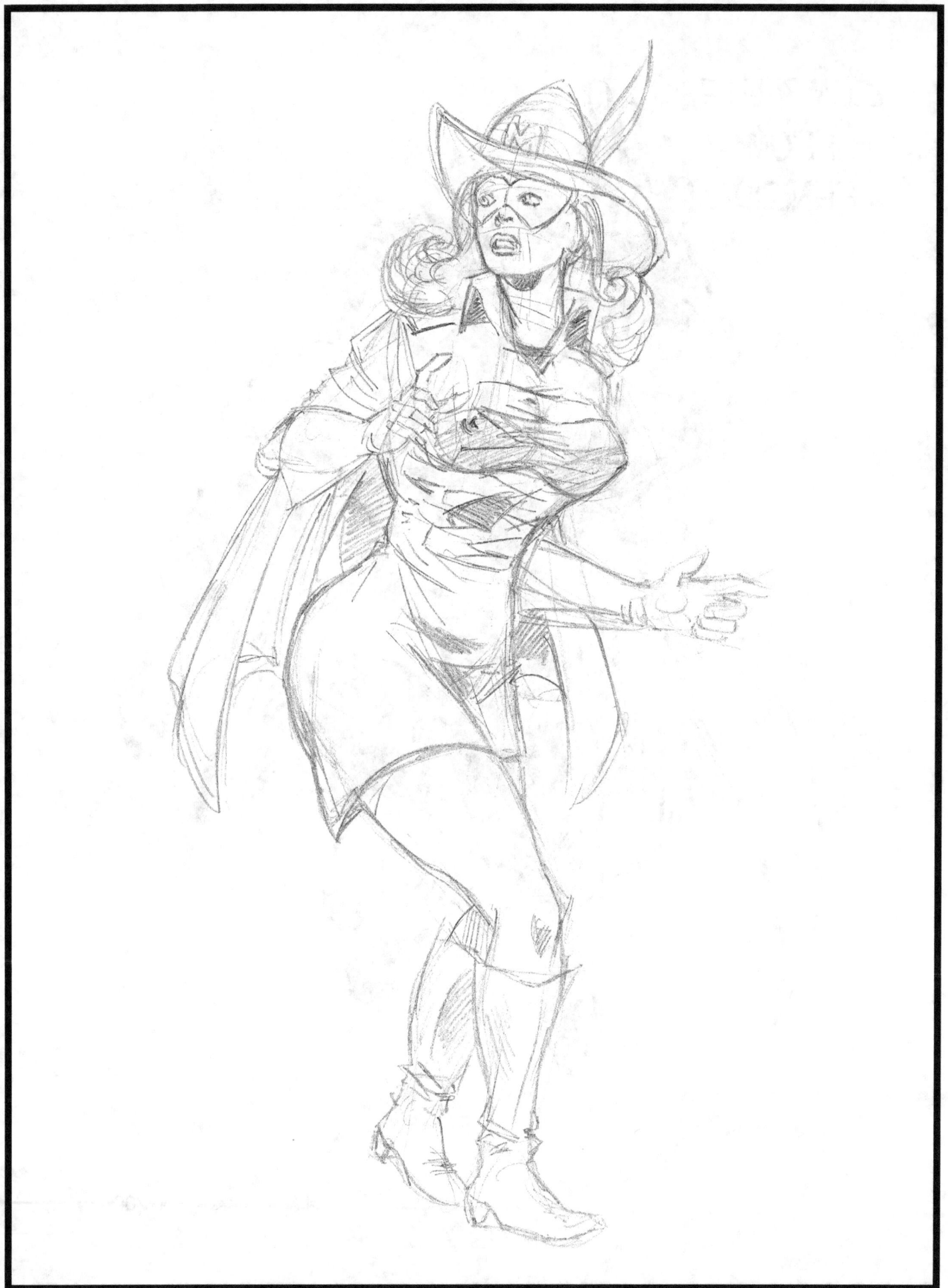

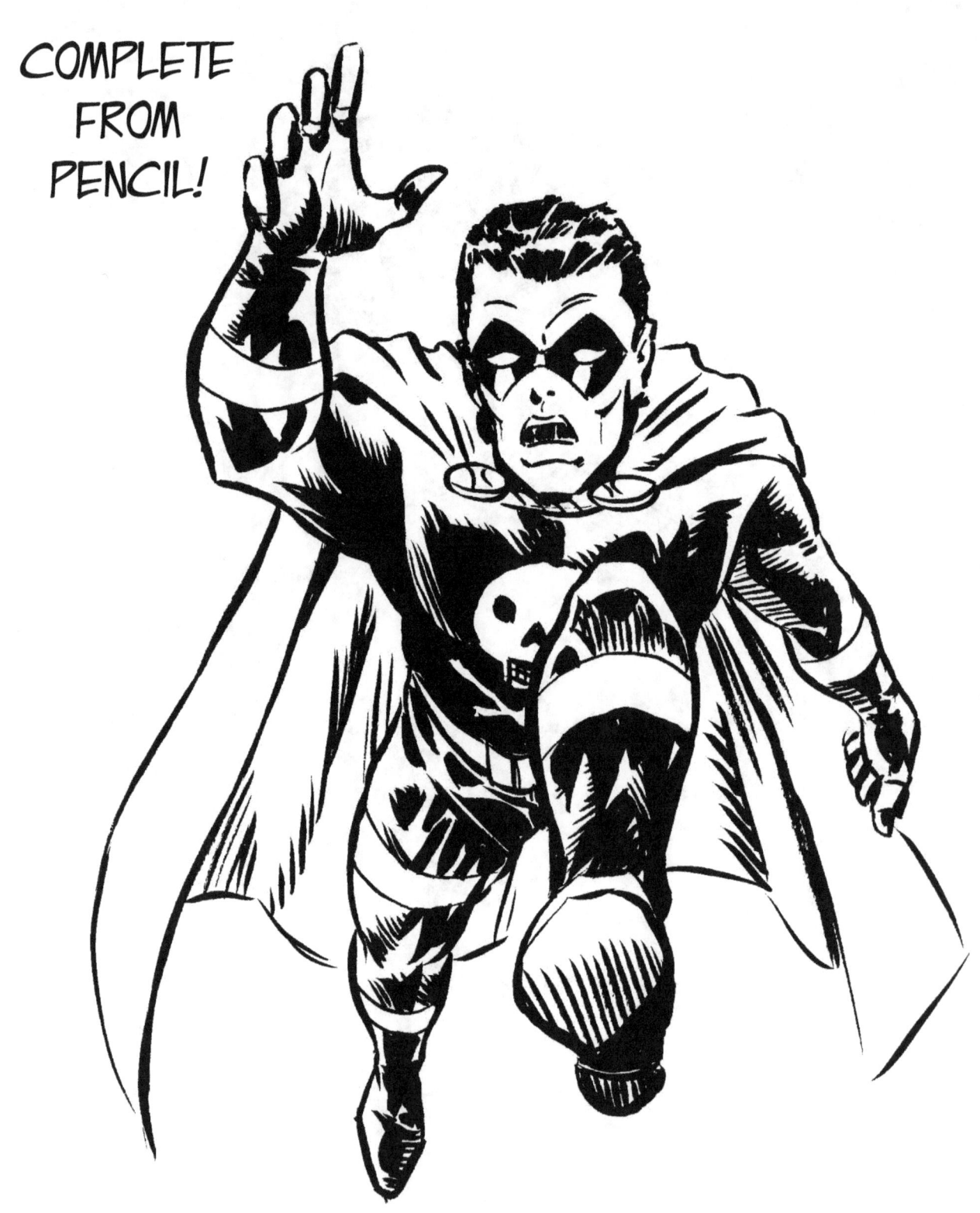

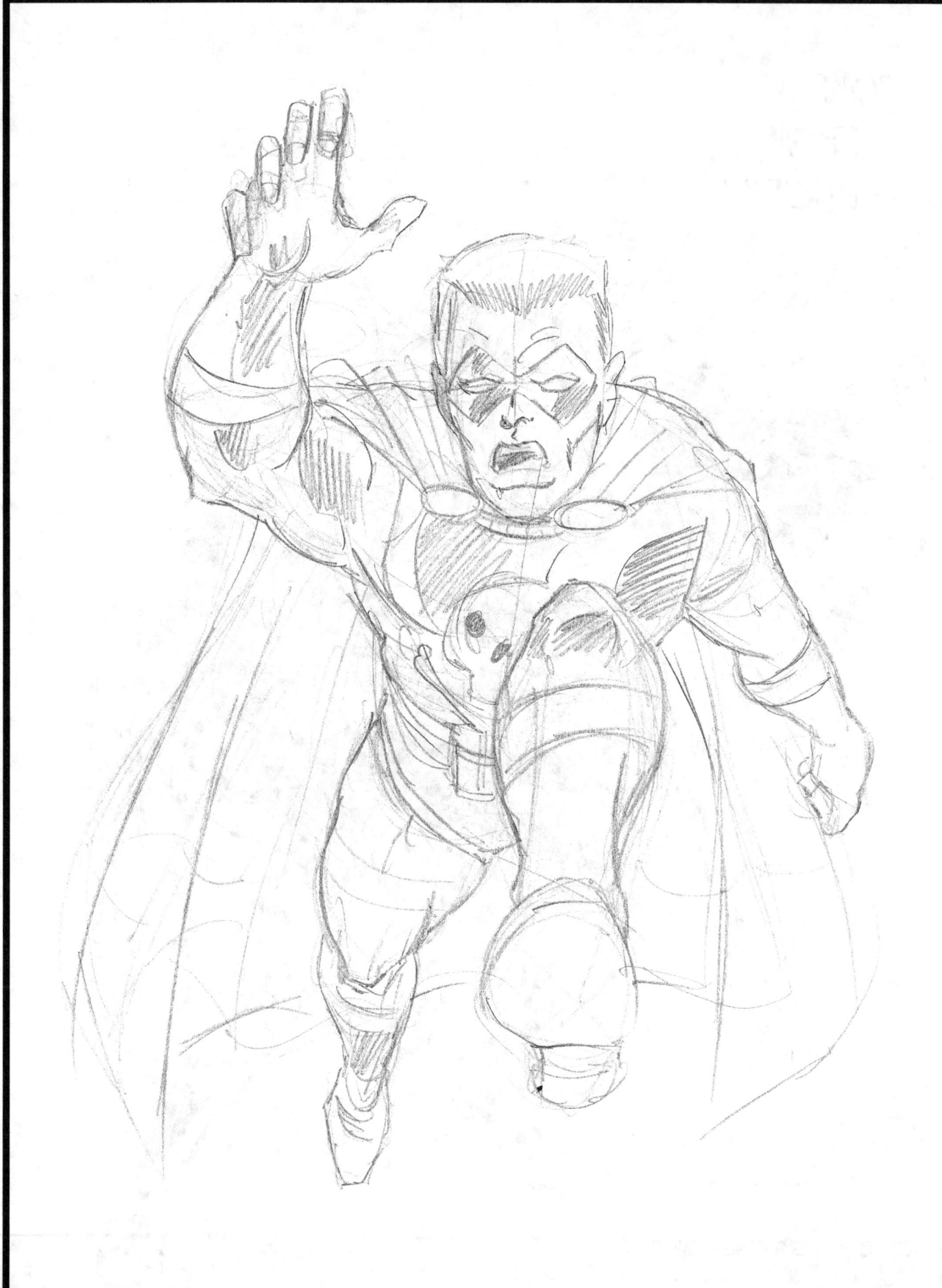

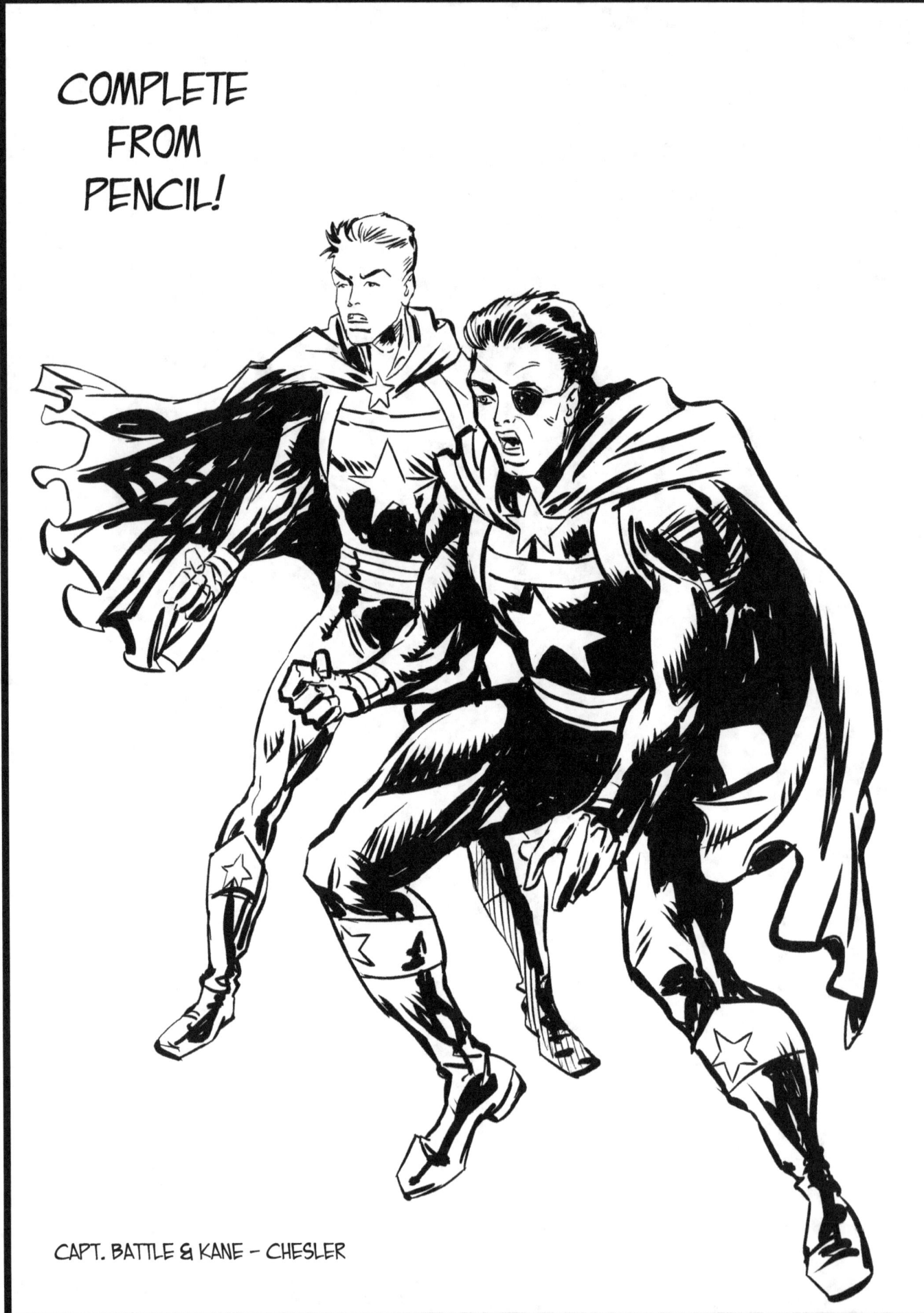

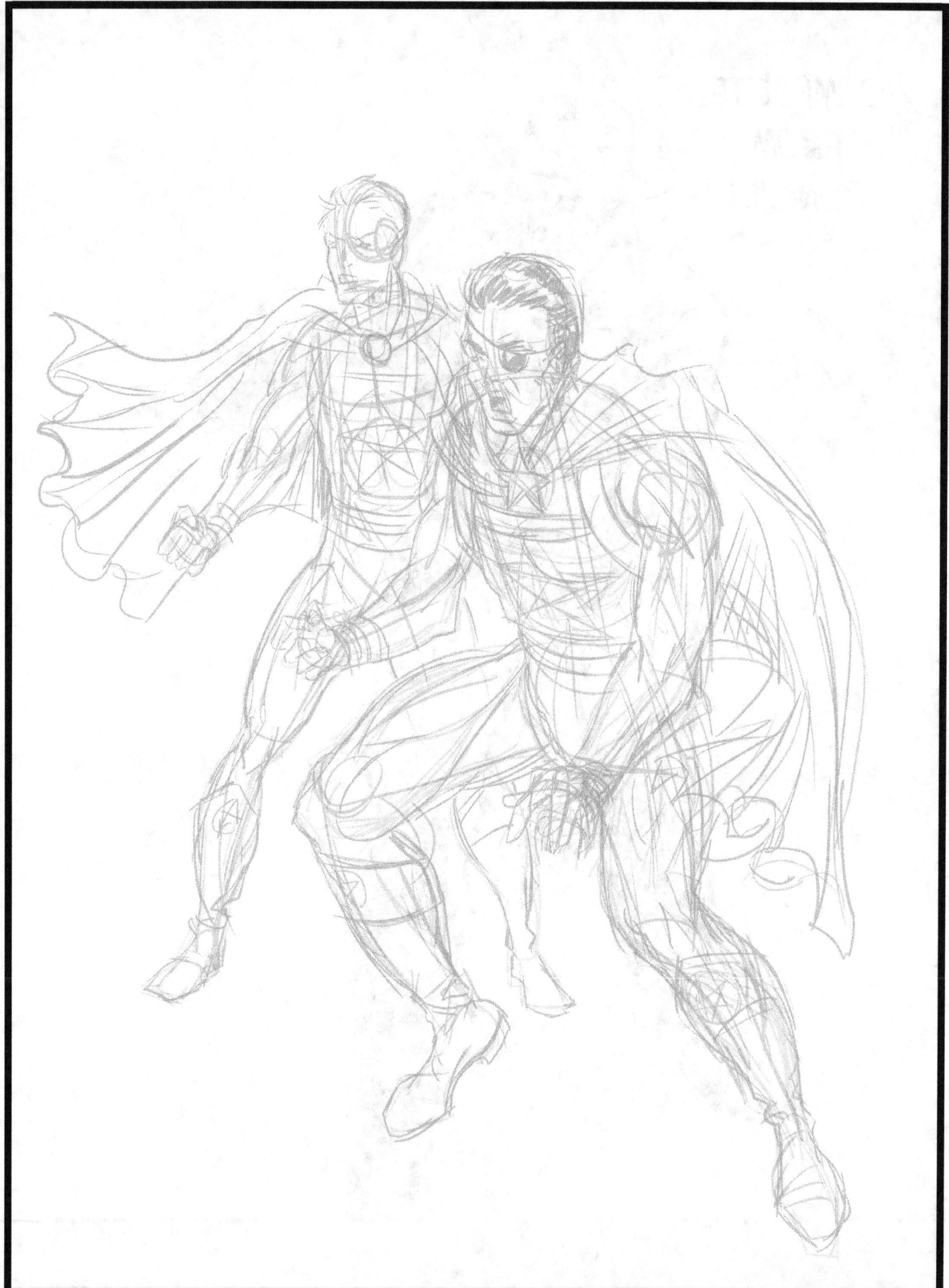

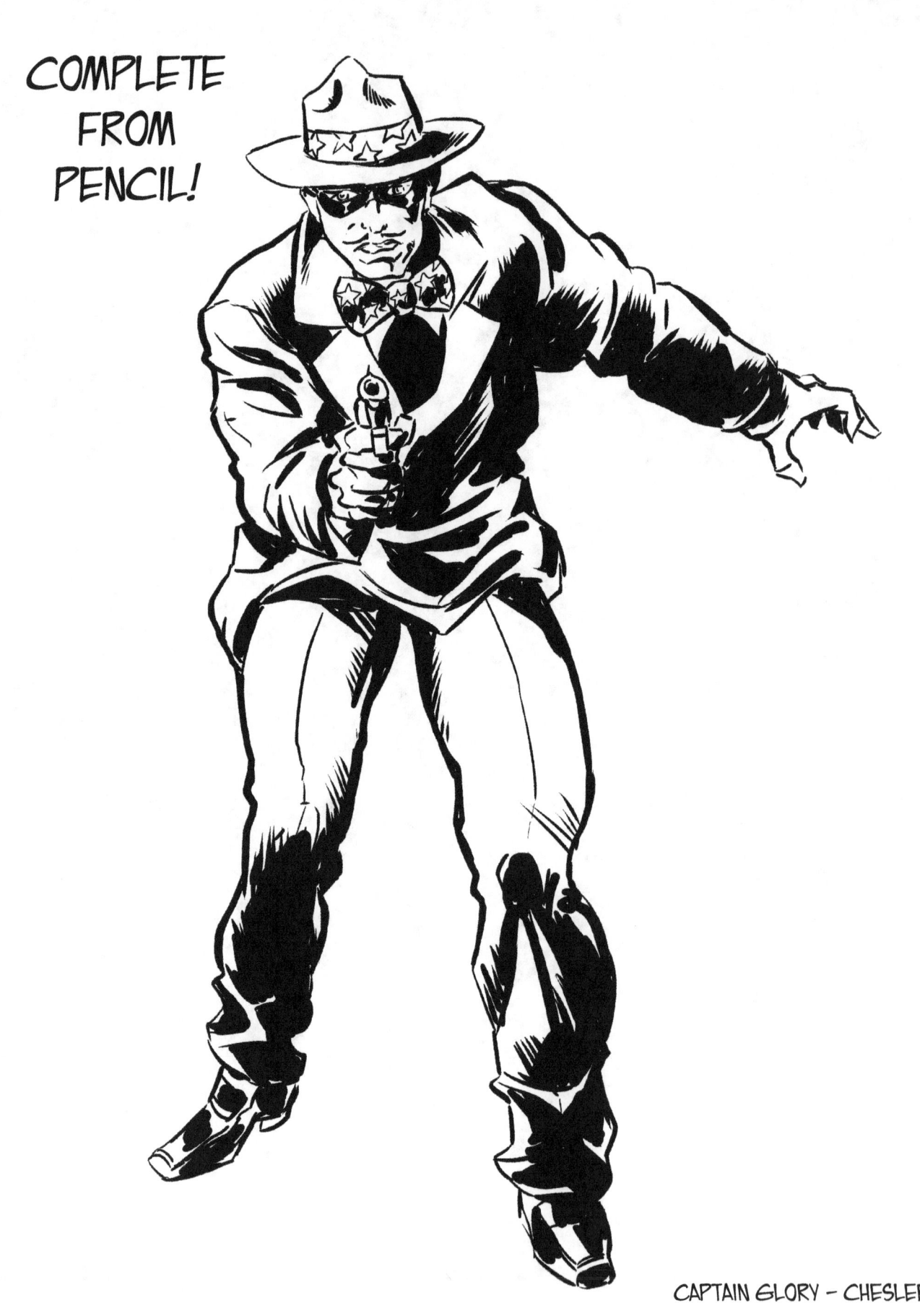

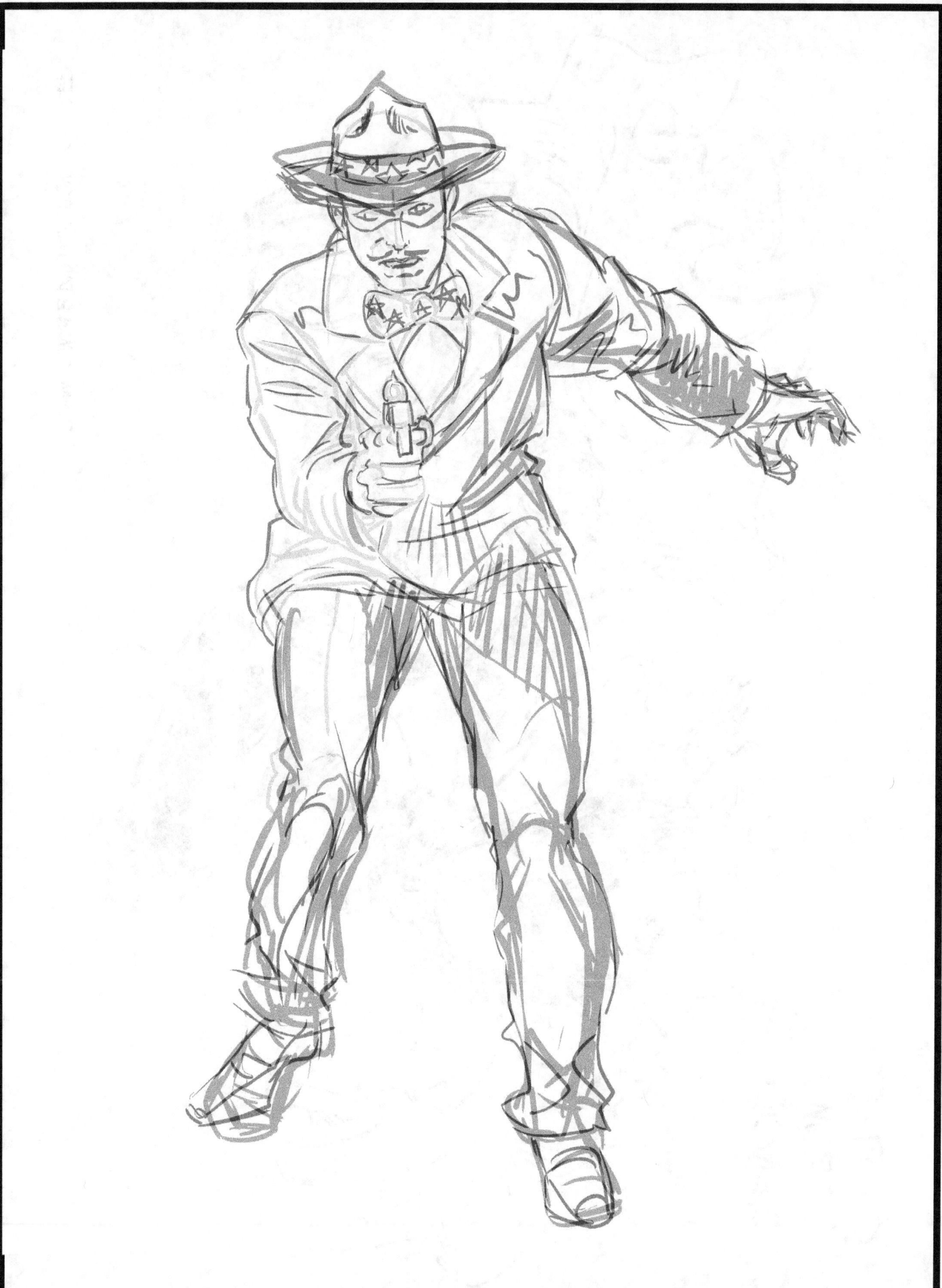

COMPLETE FROM PENCIL!

DYNAMIC MAN & DYNAMIC BOY – CHESLER

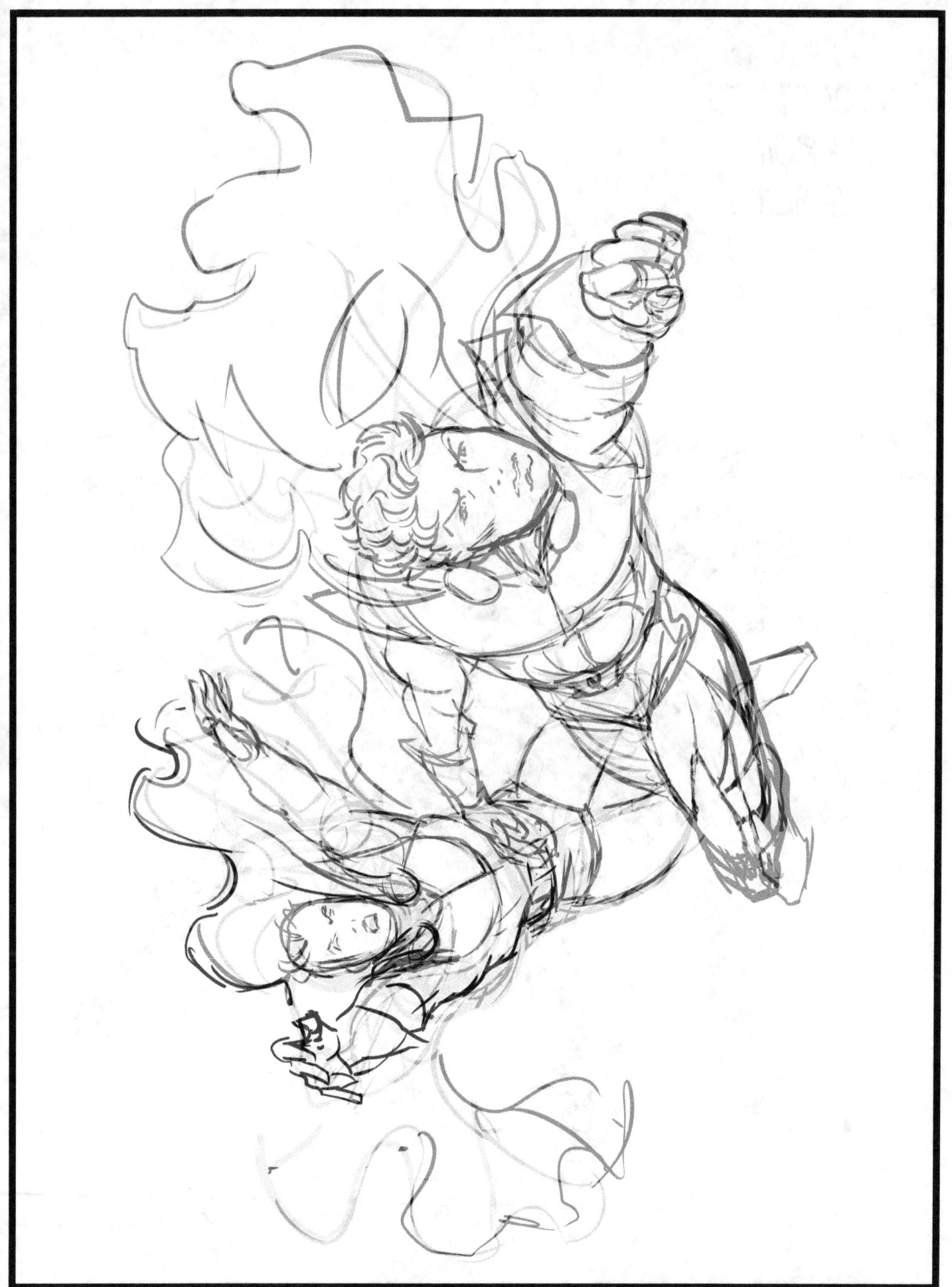

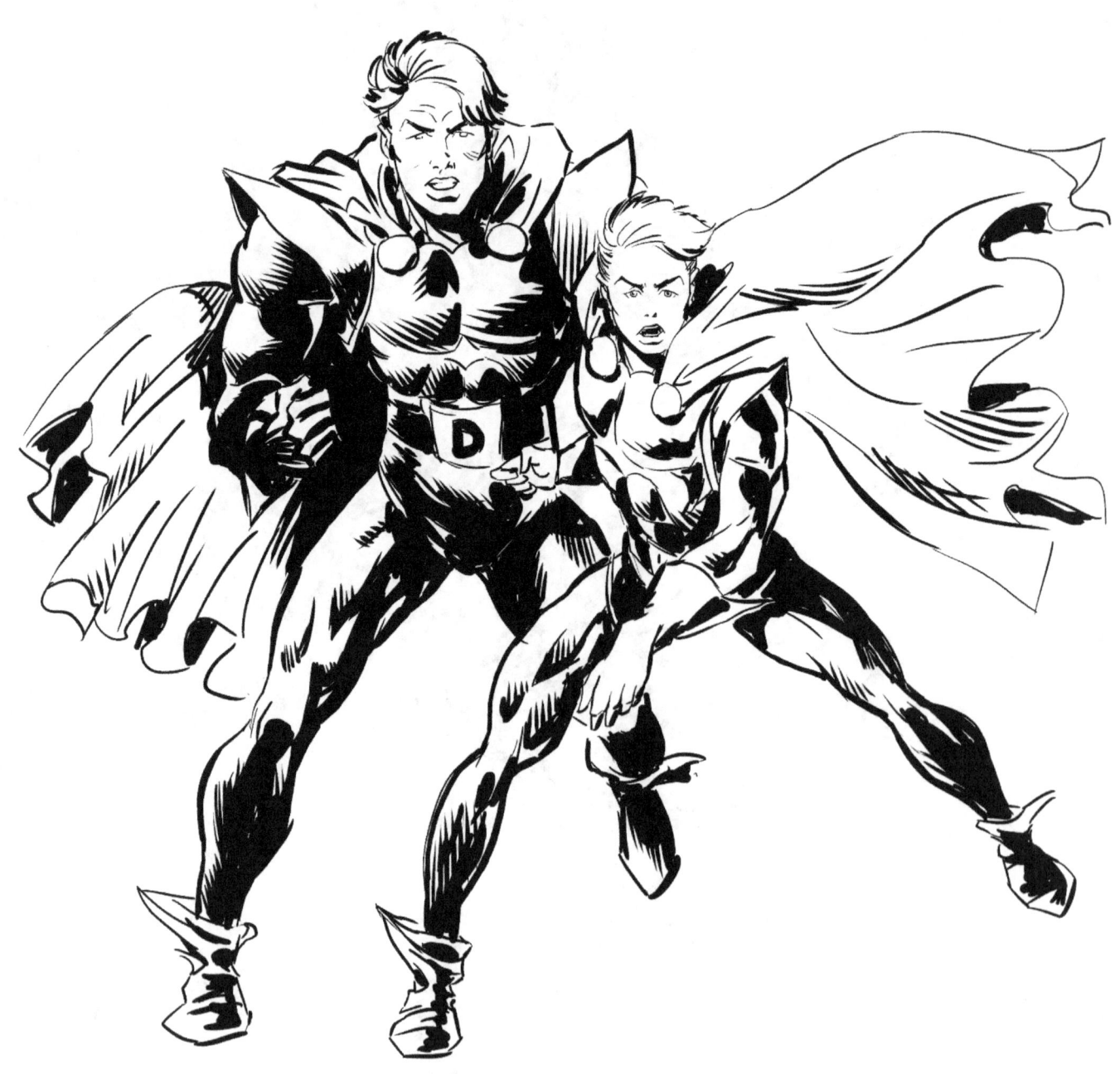

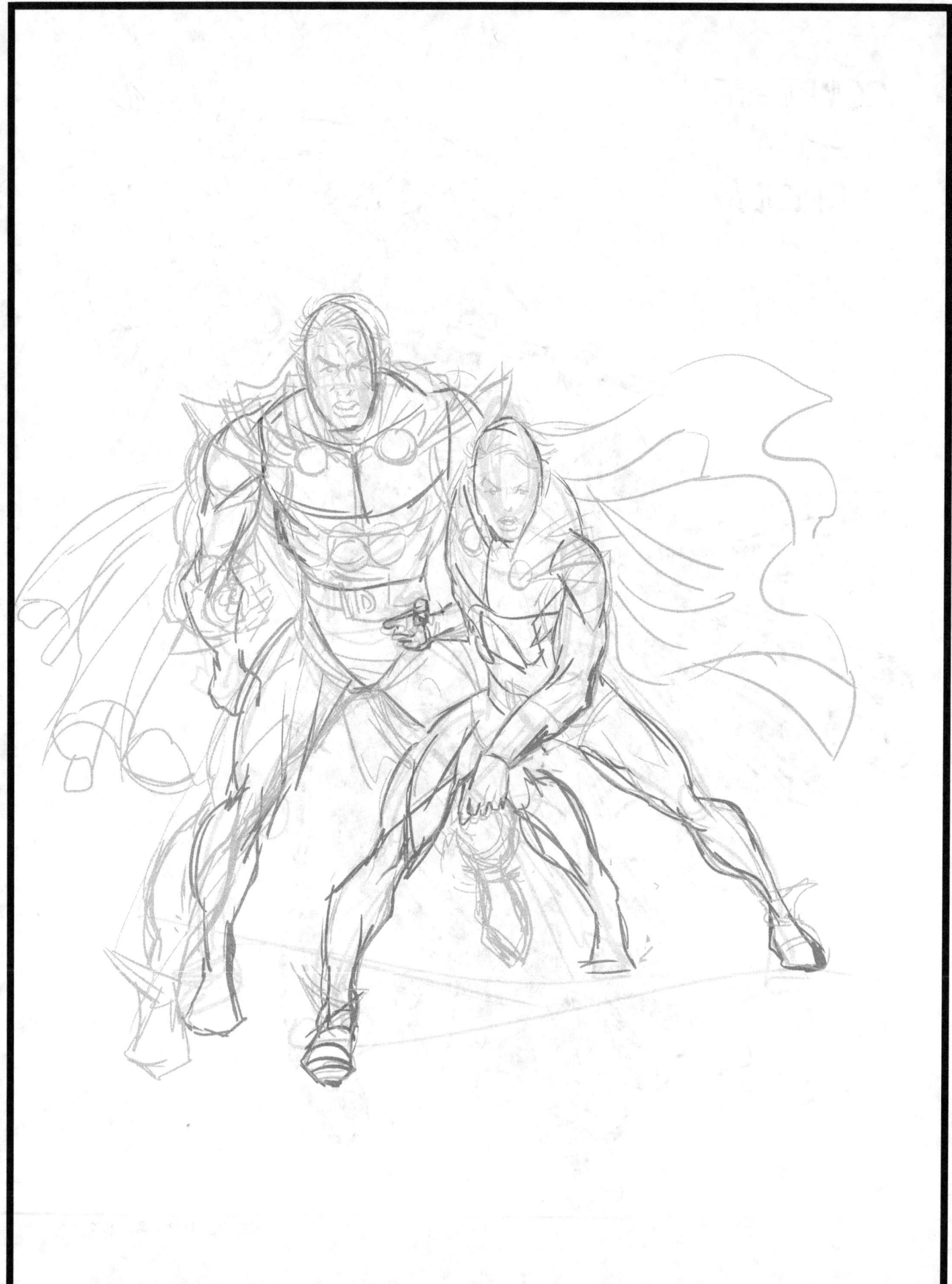

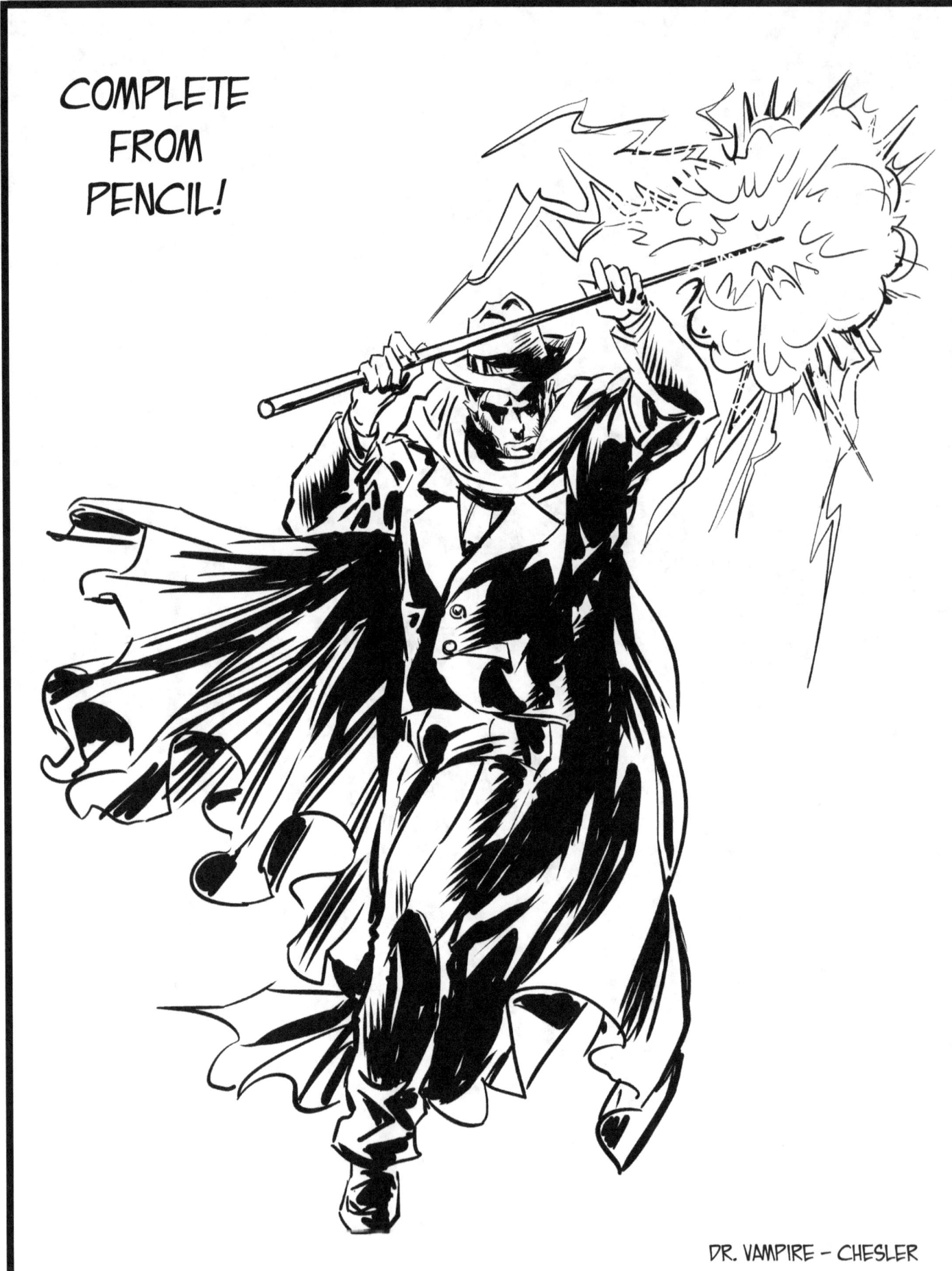

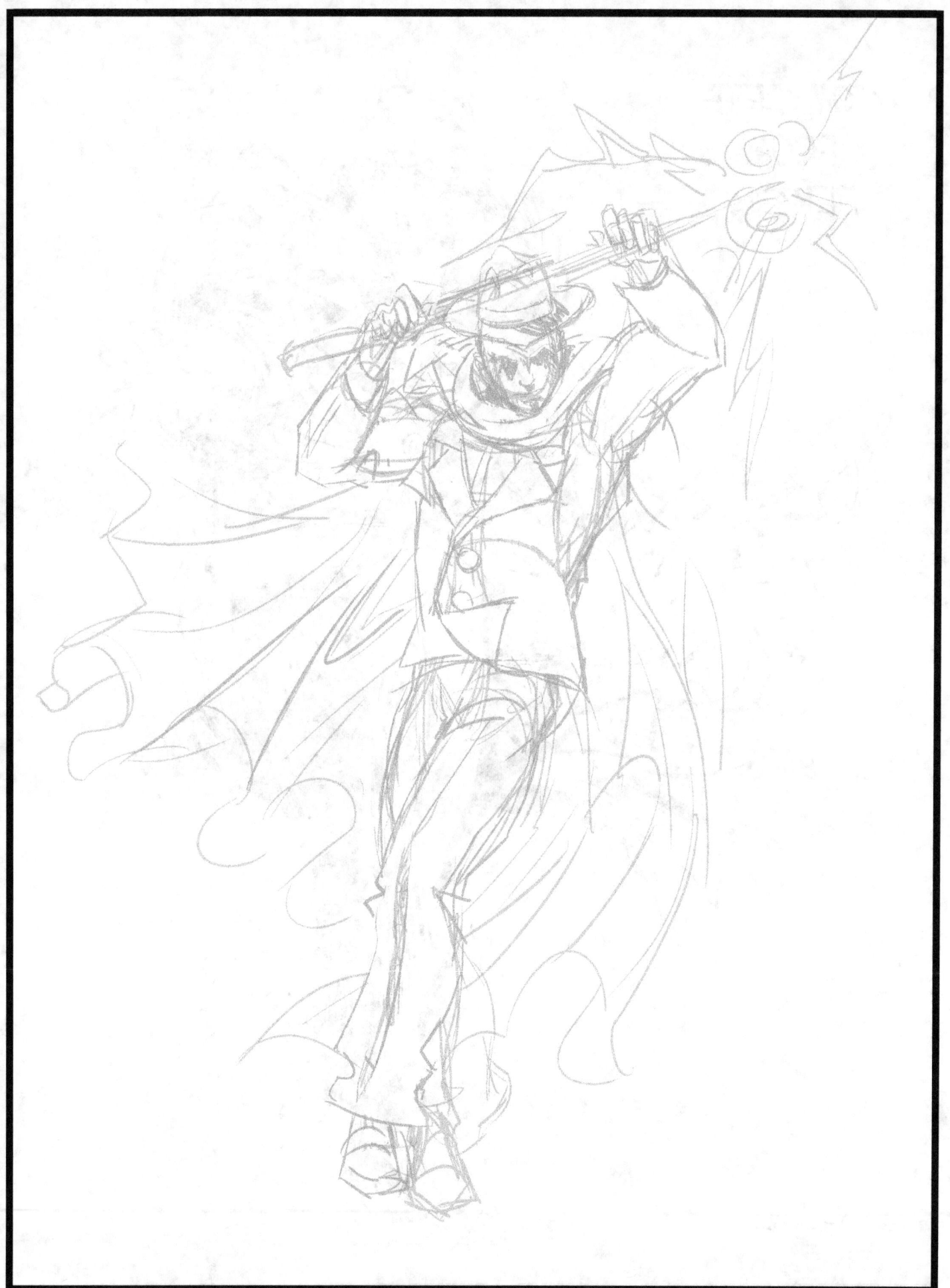

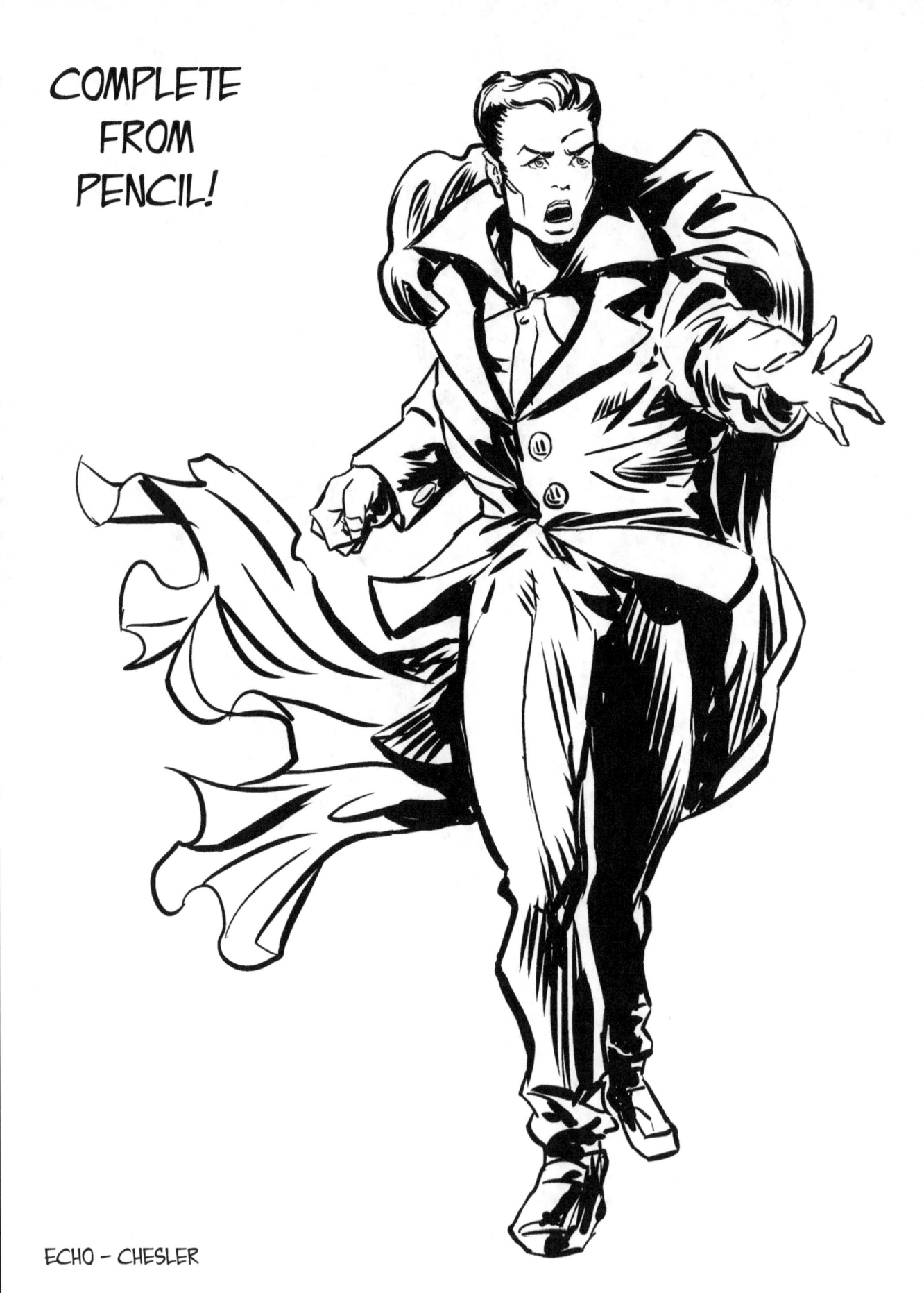

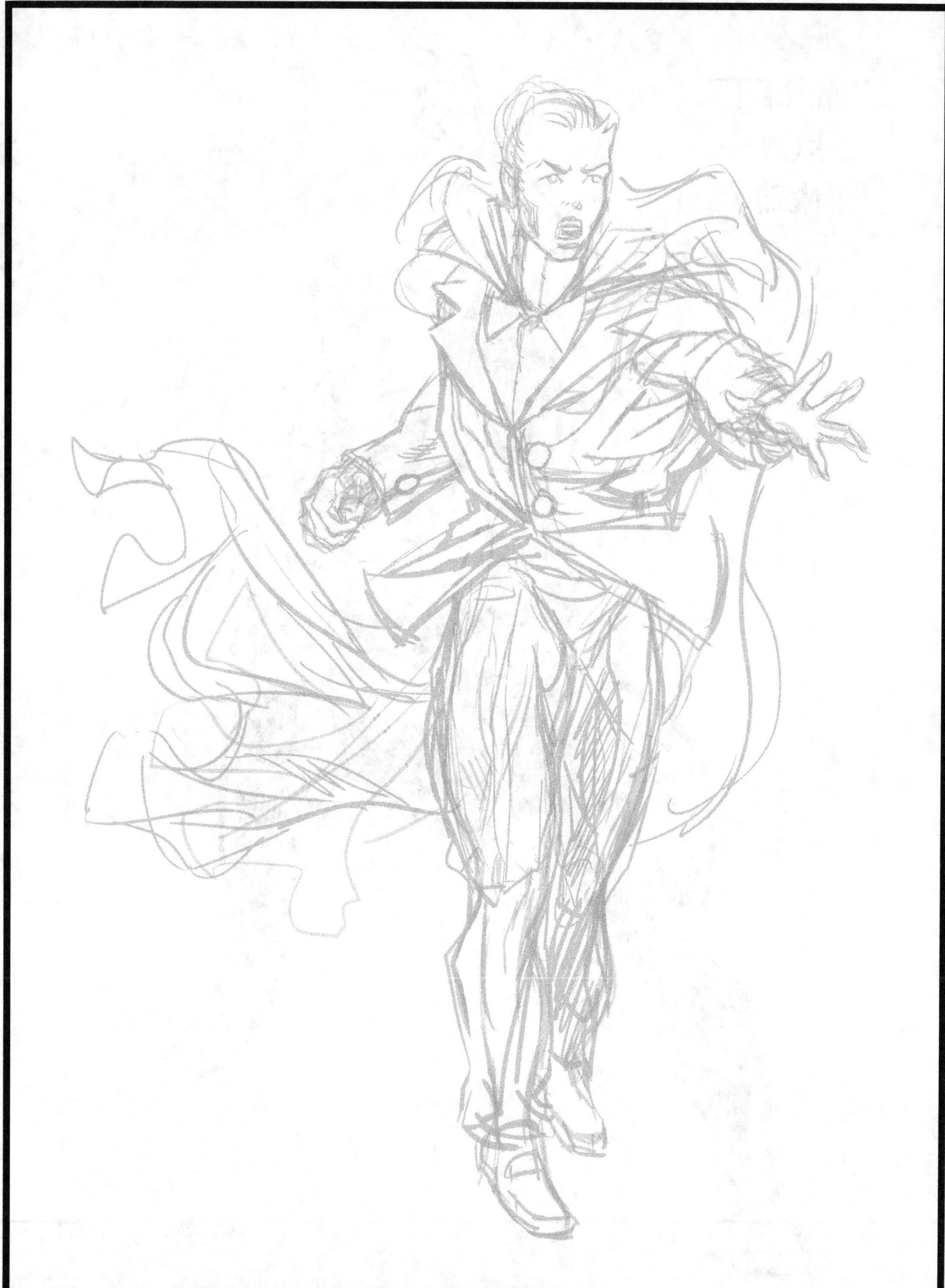

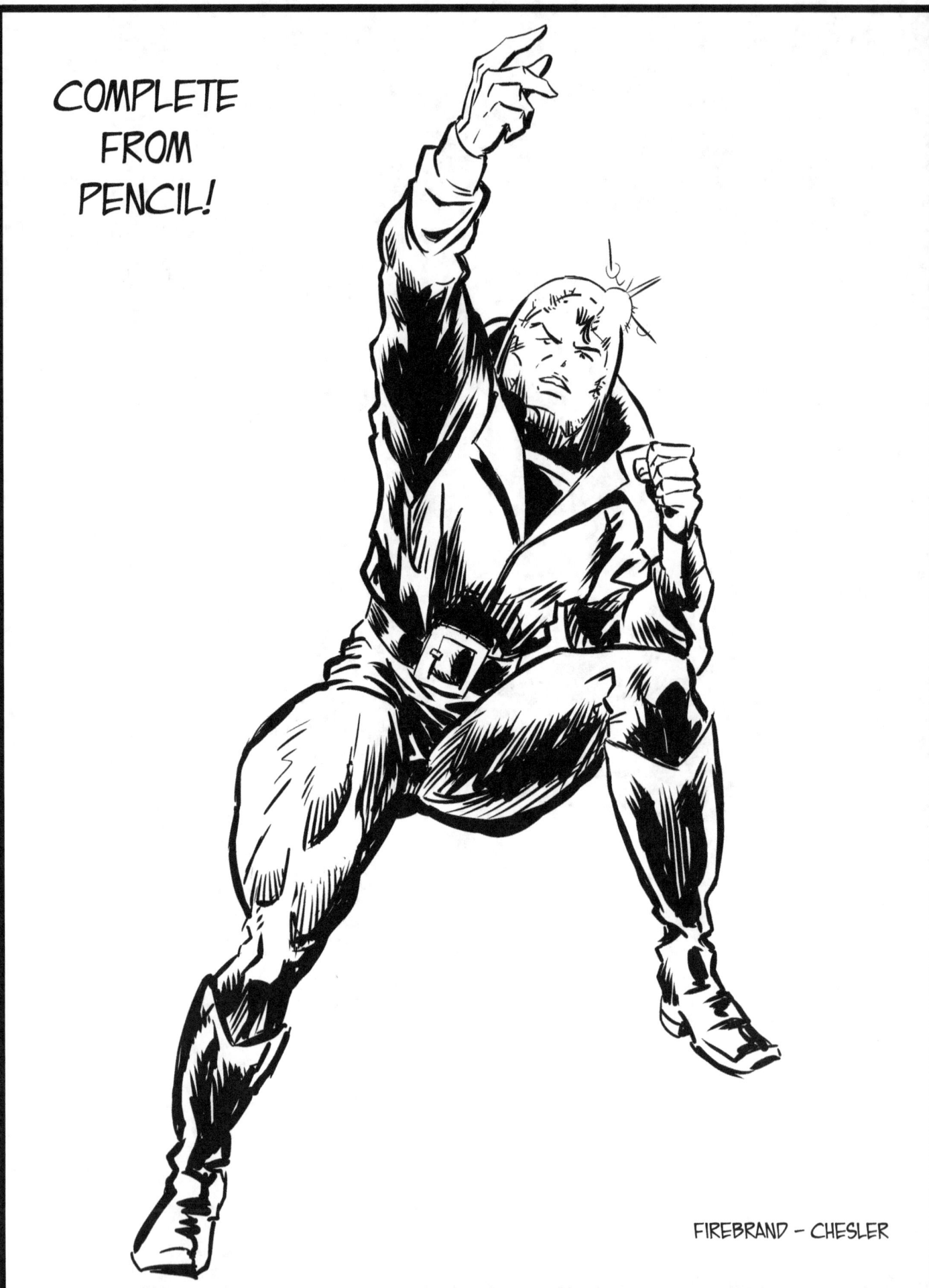

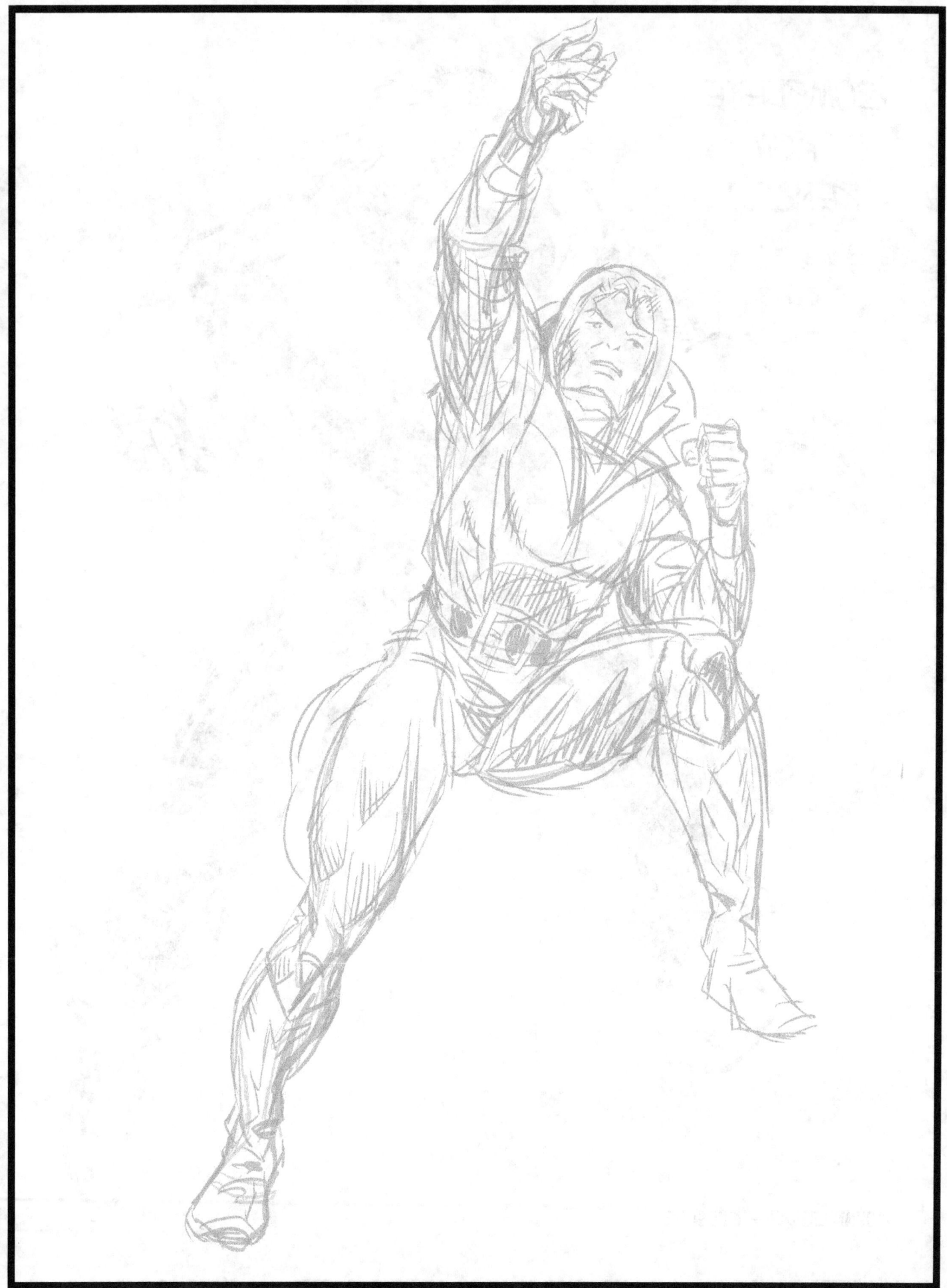

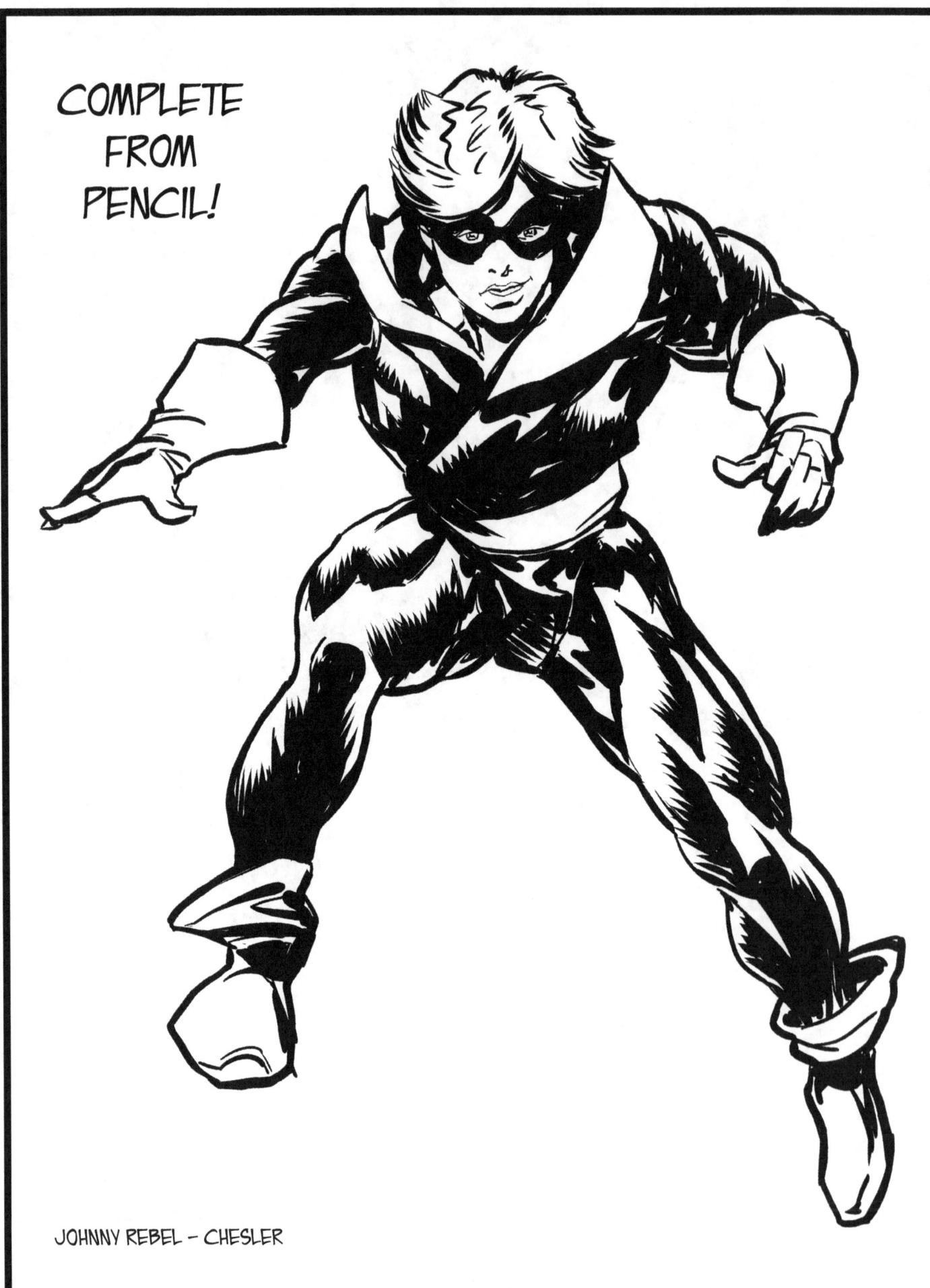

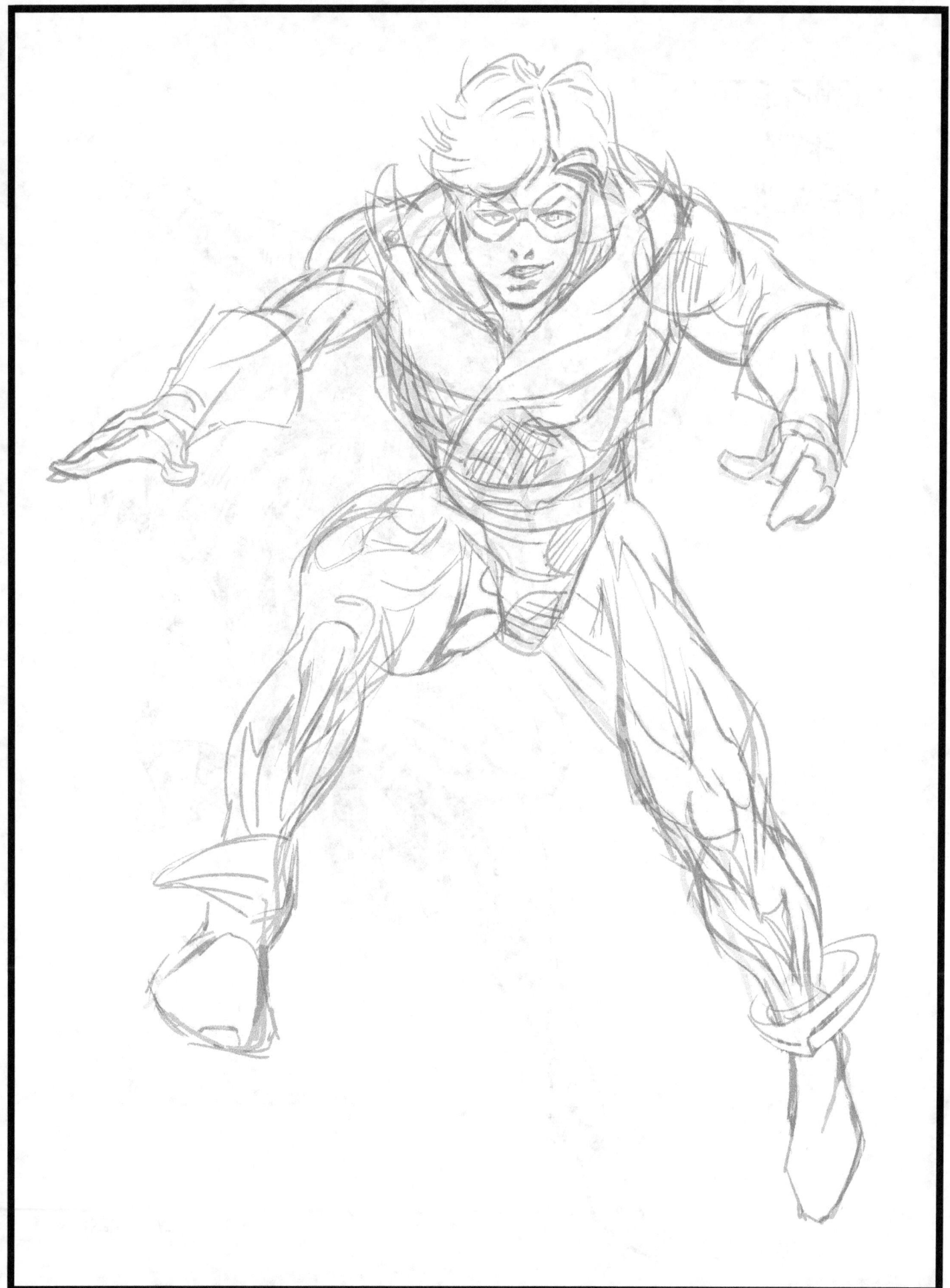

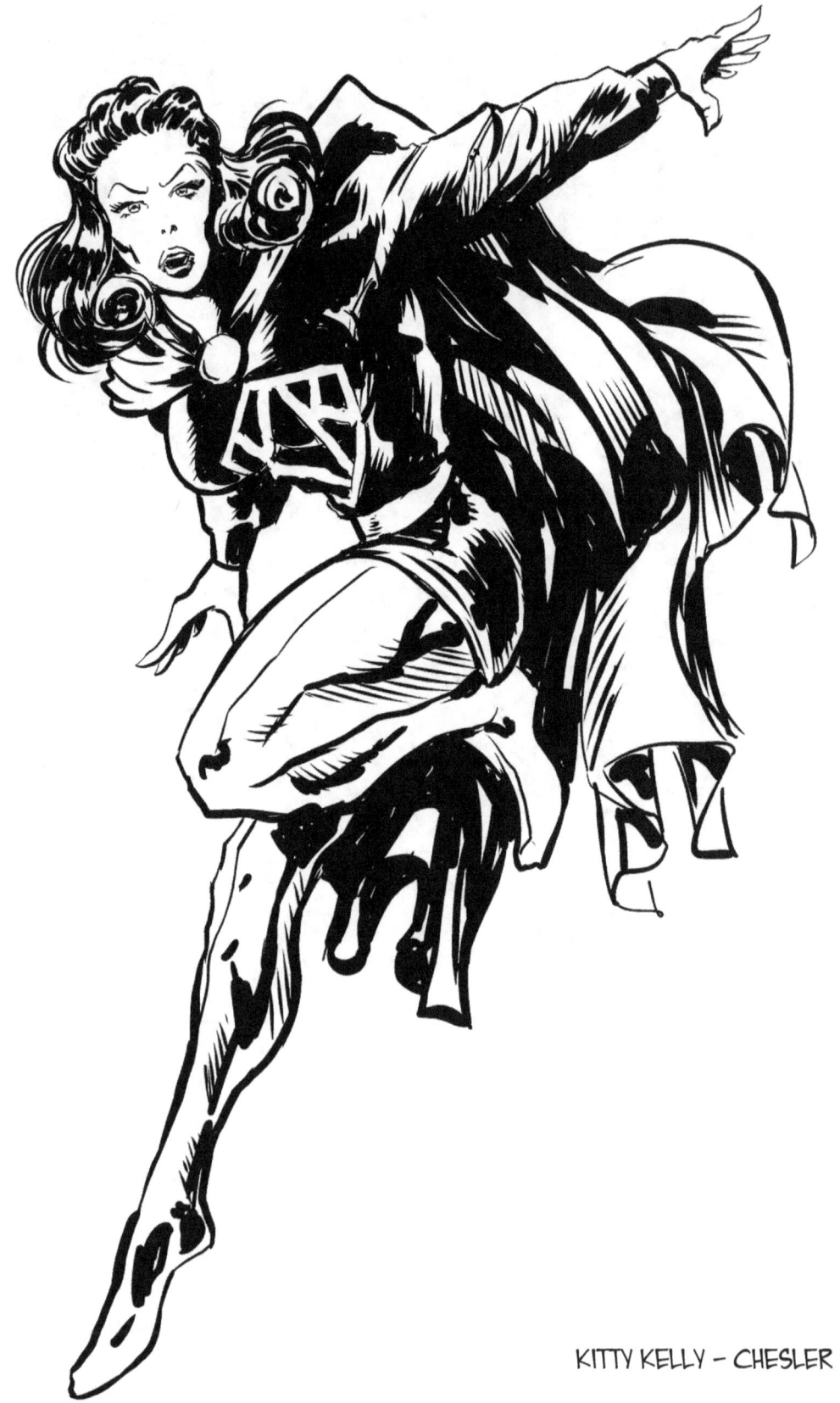

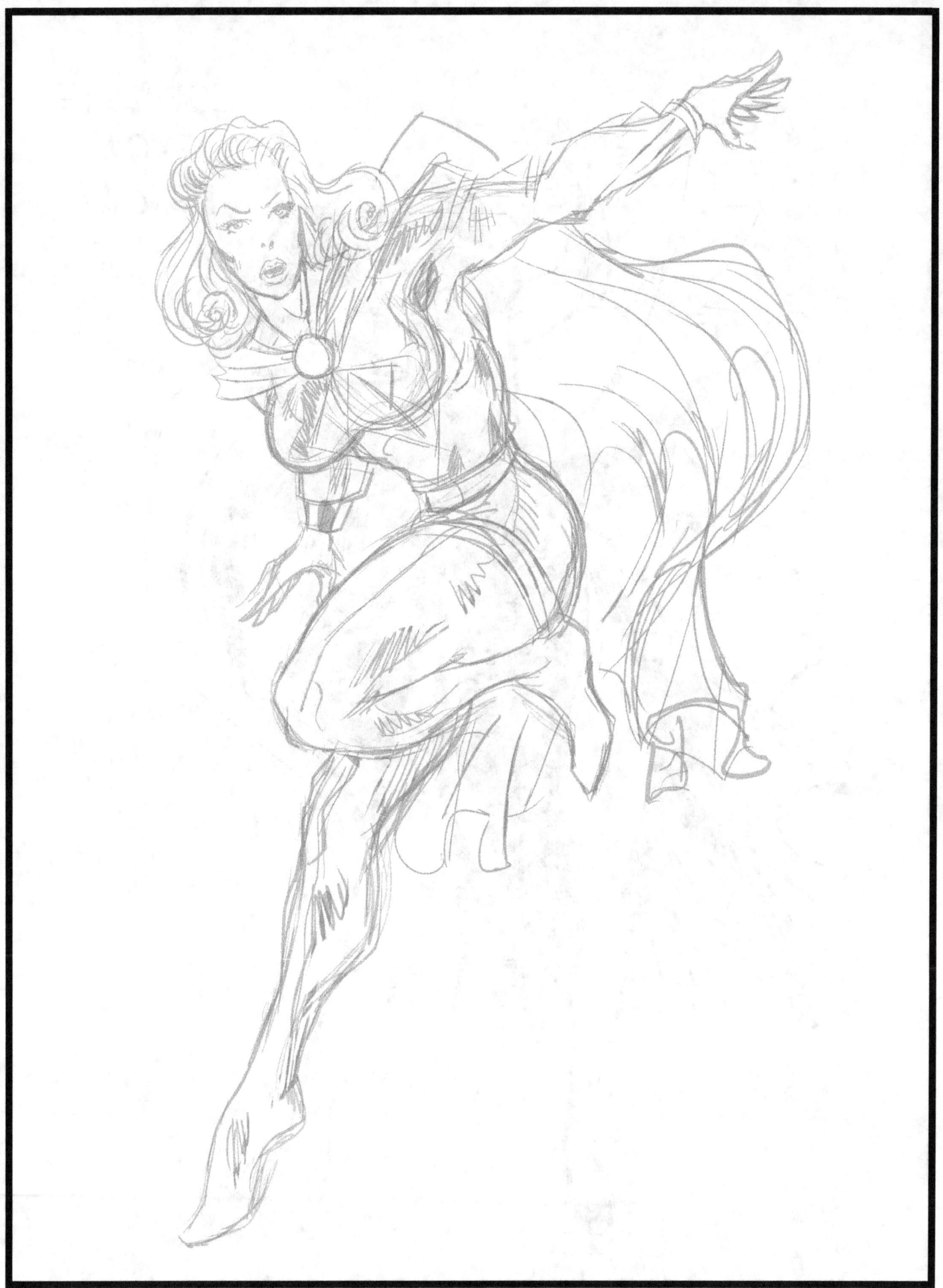

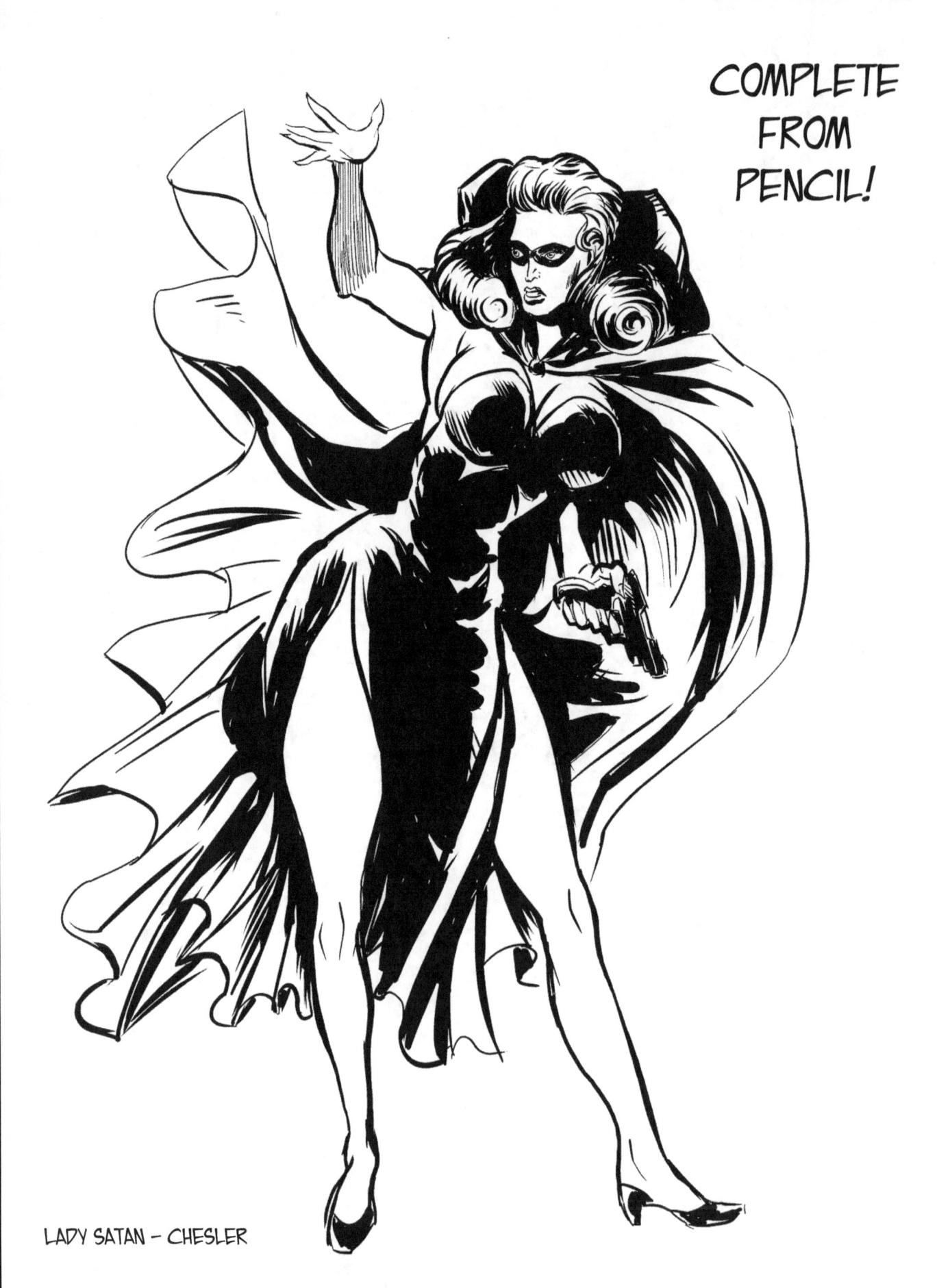

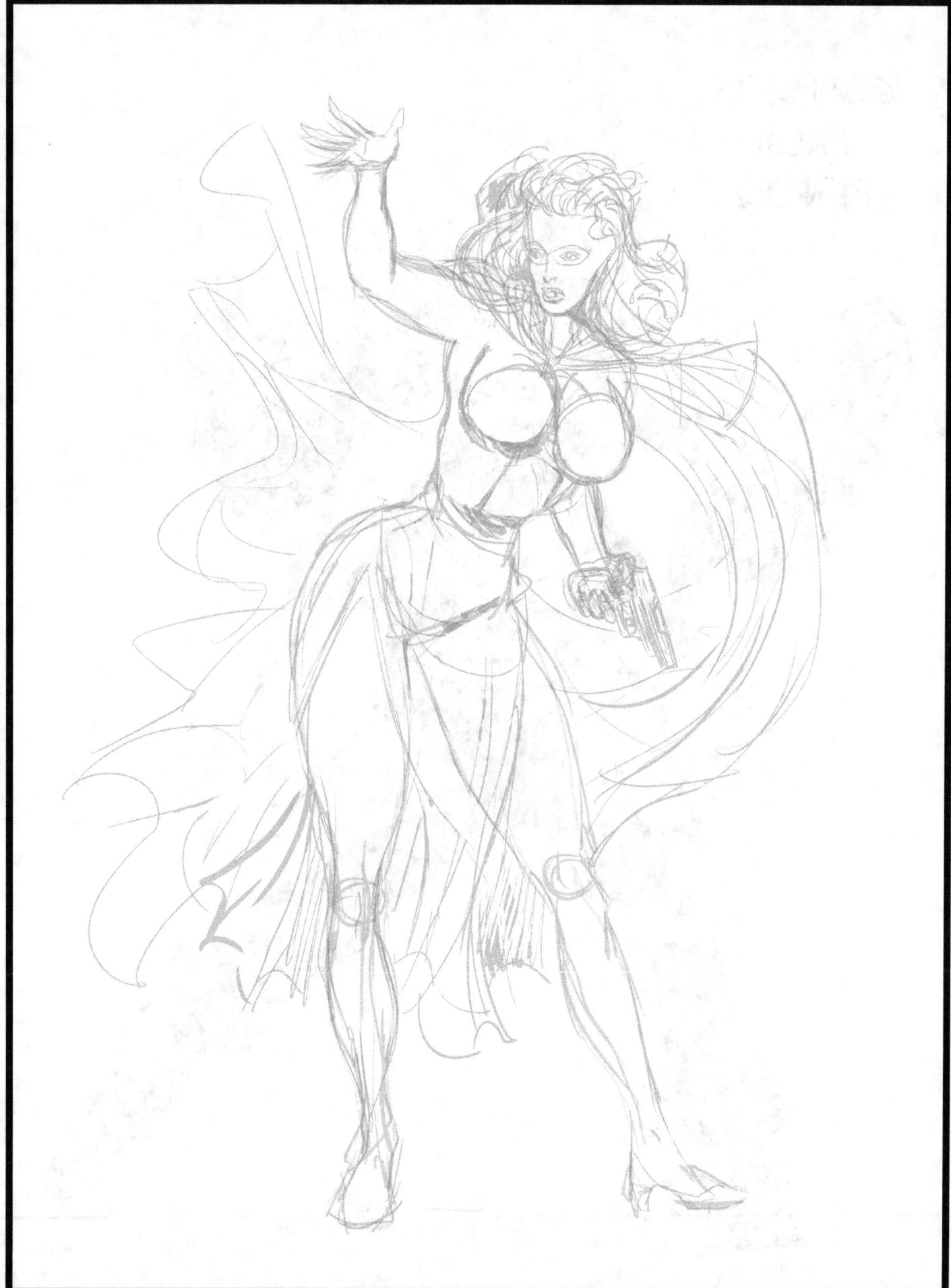

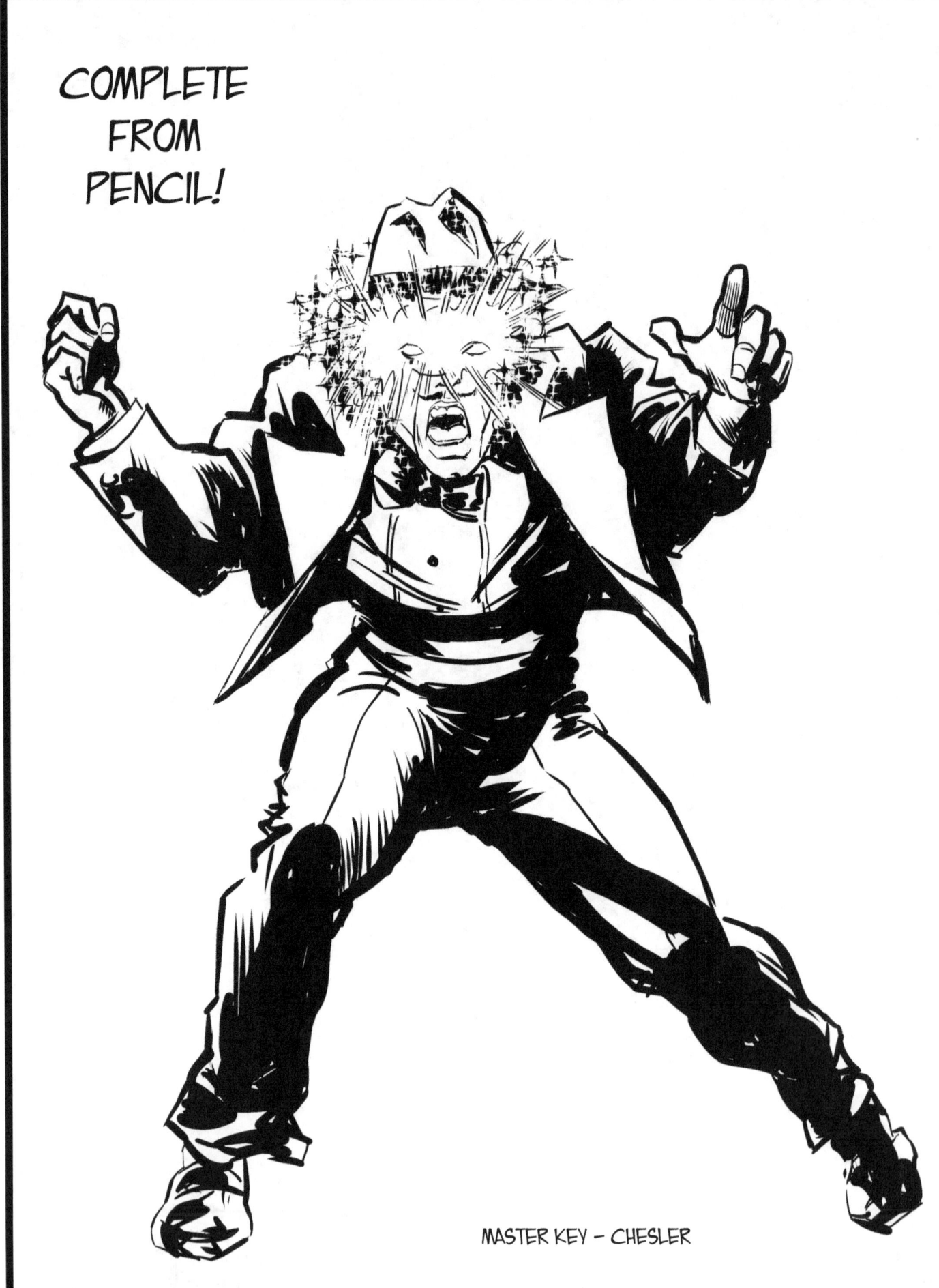

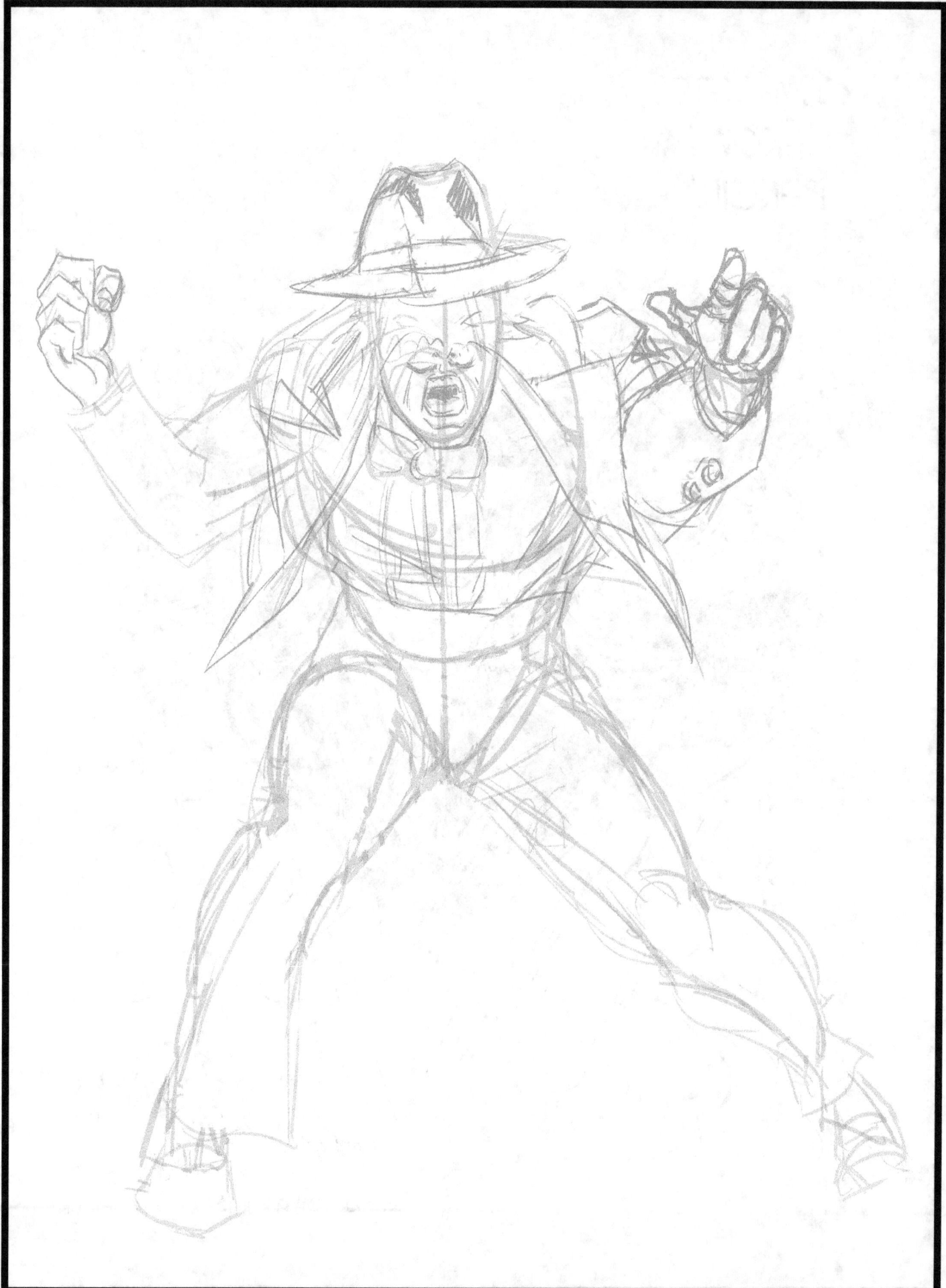

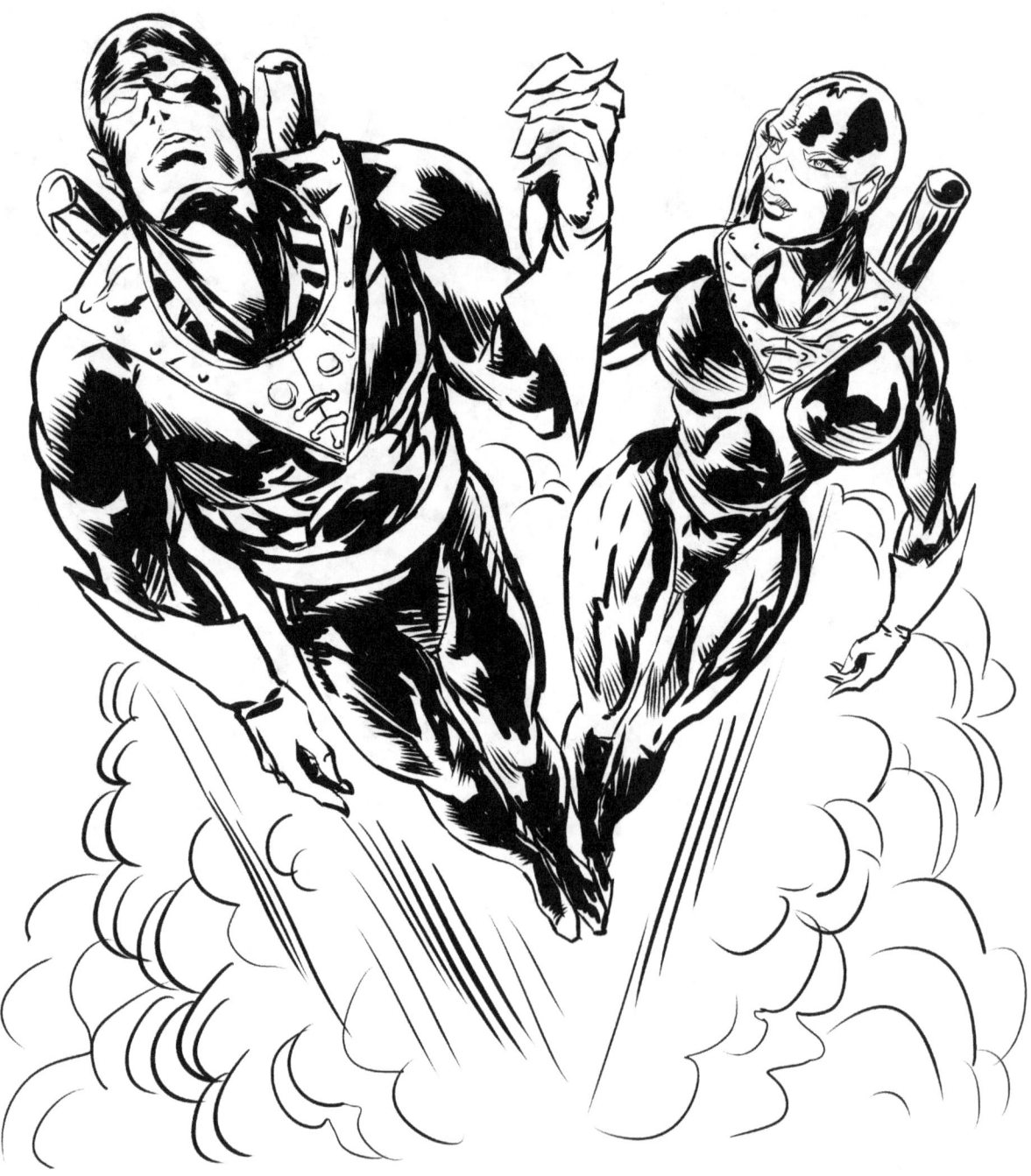

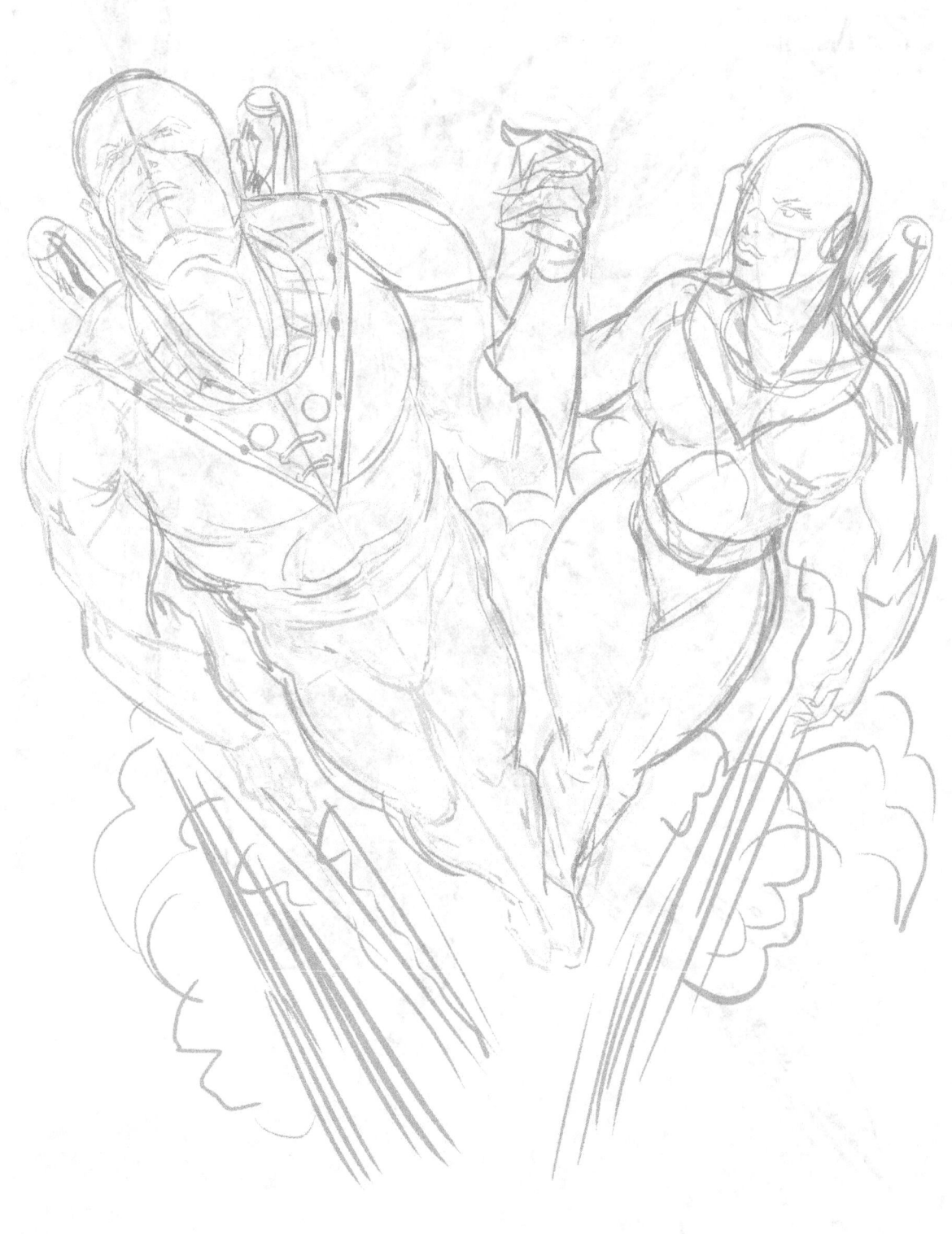

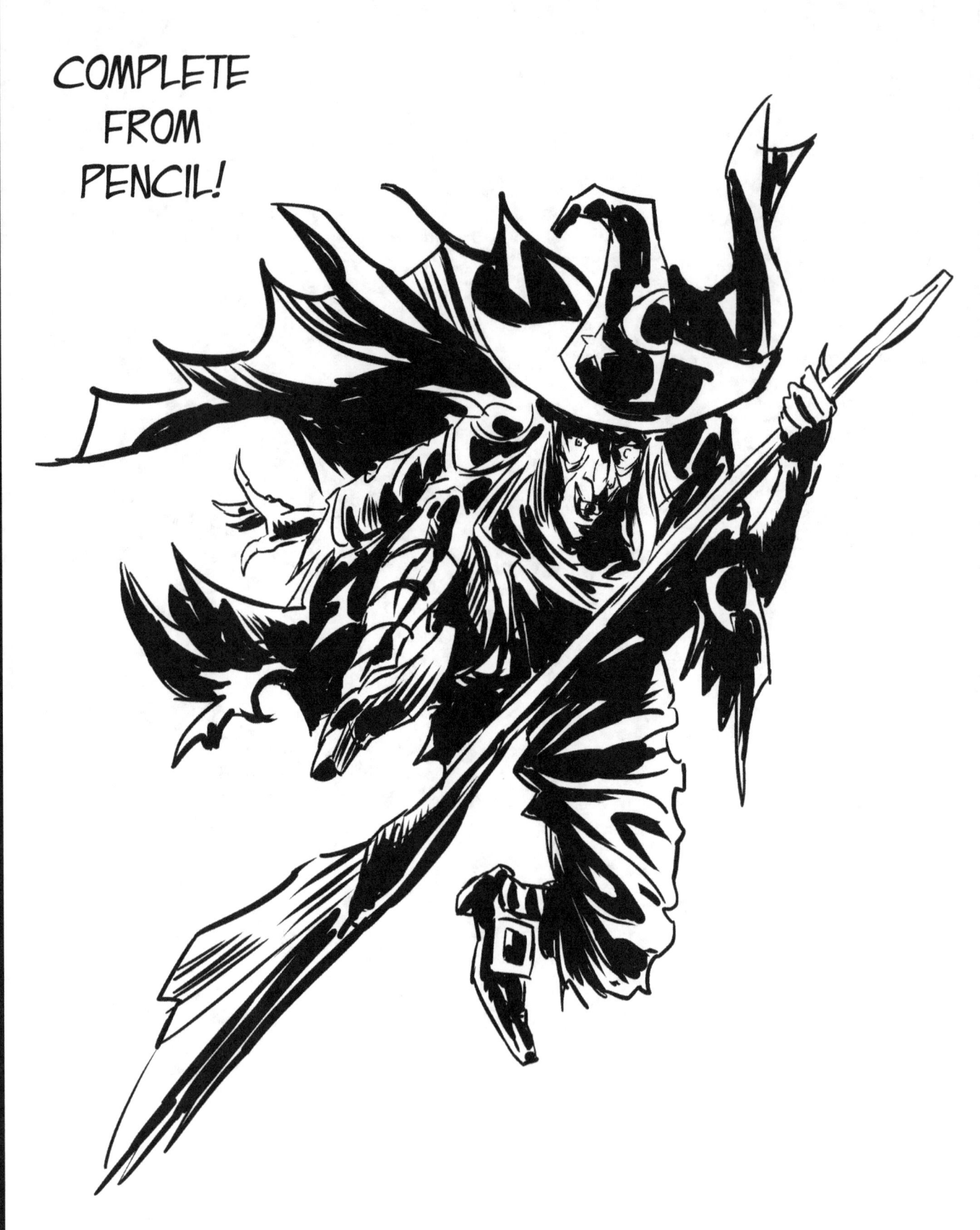

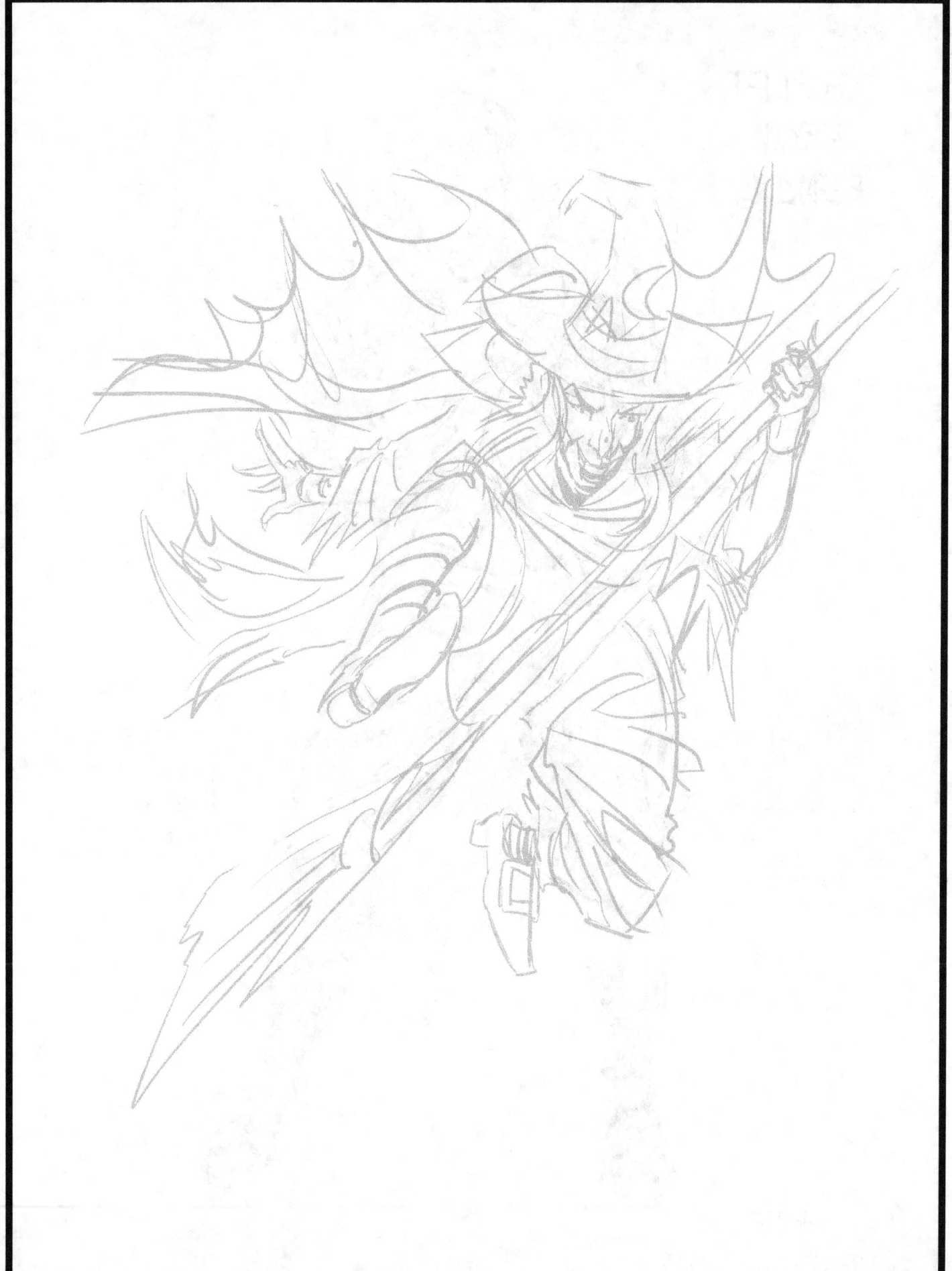

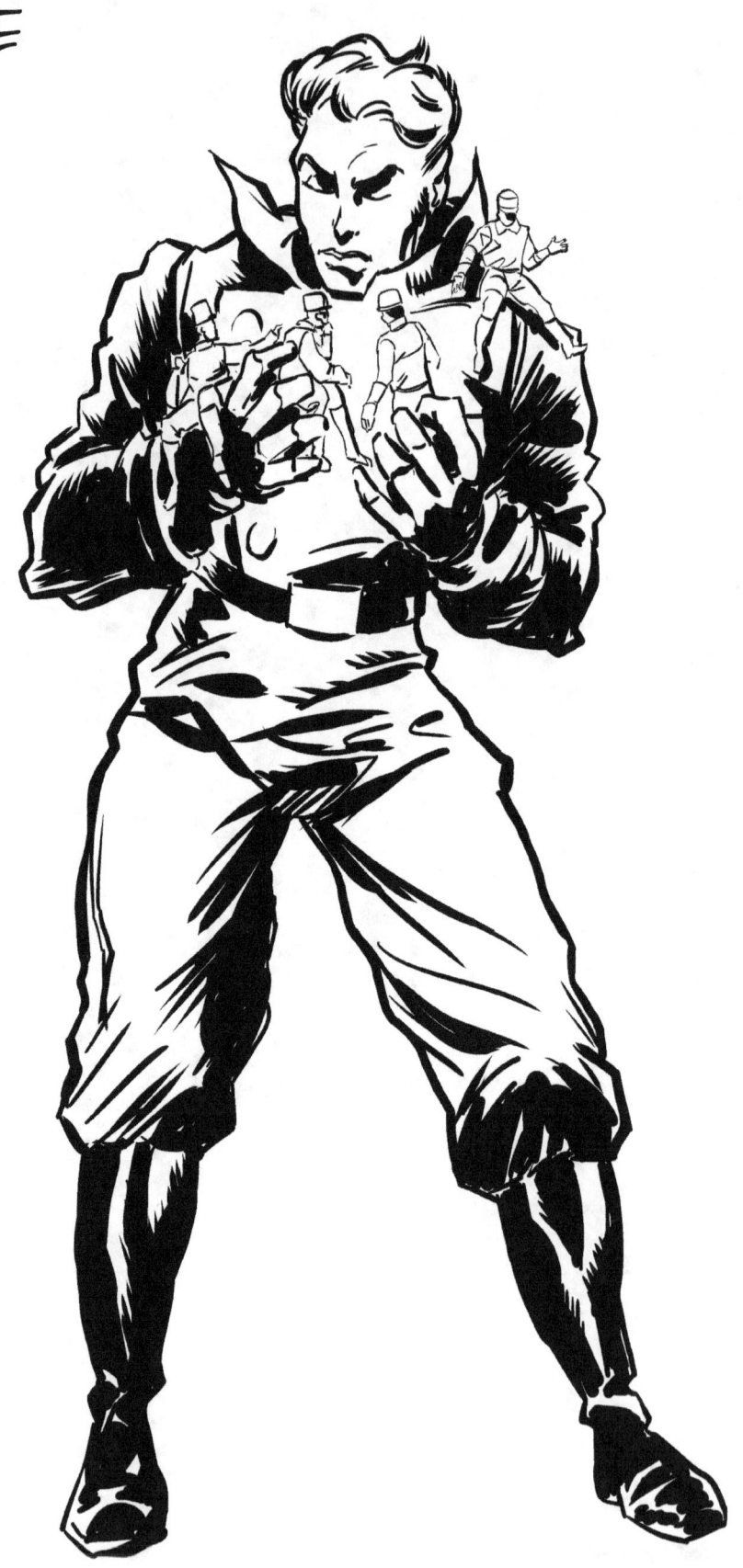

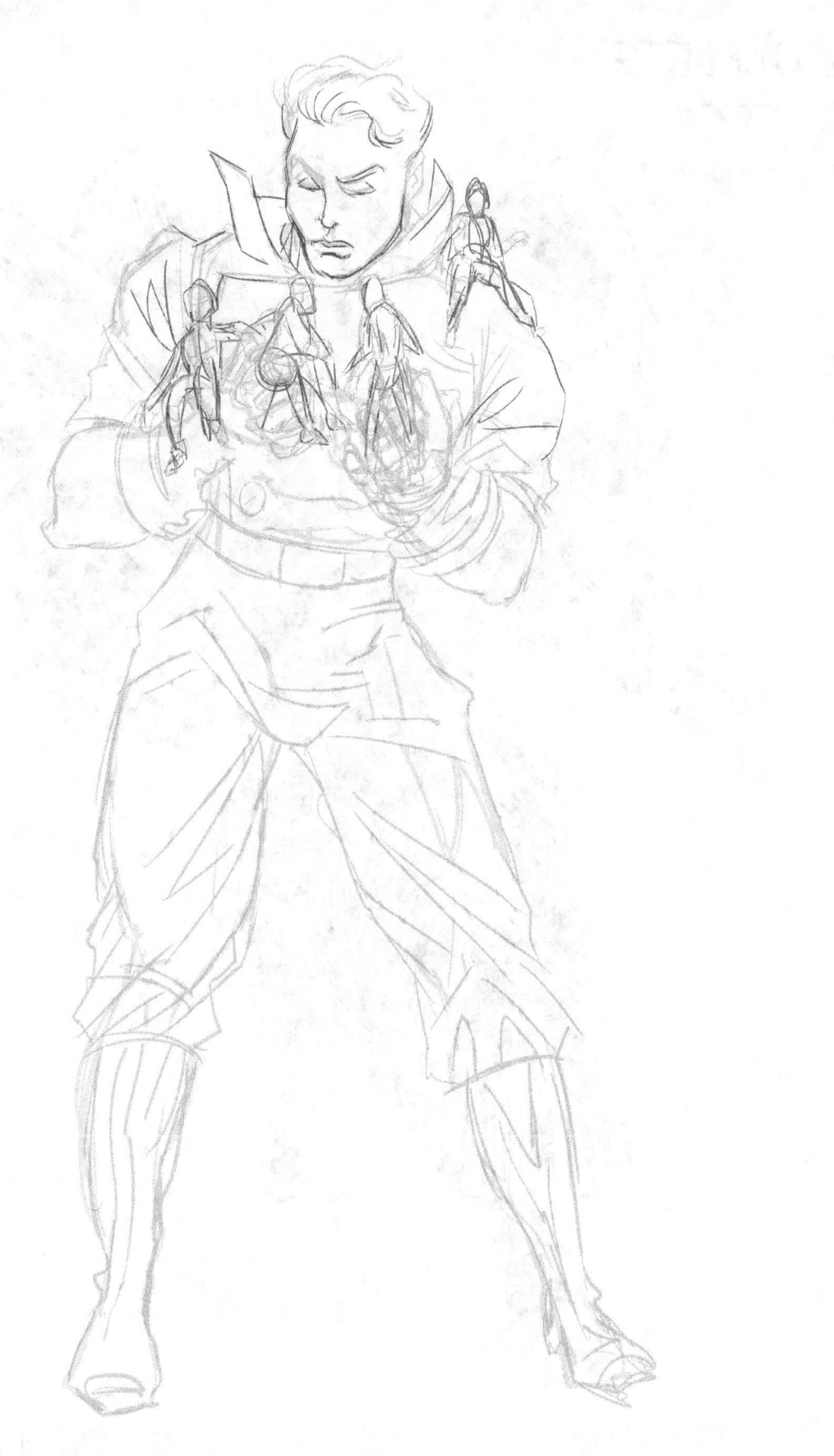

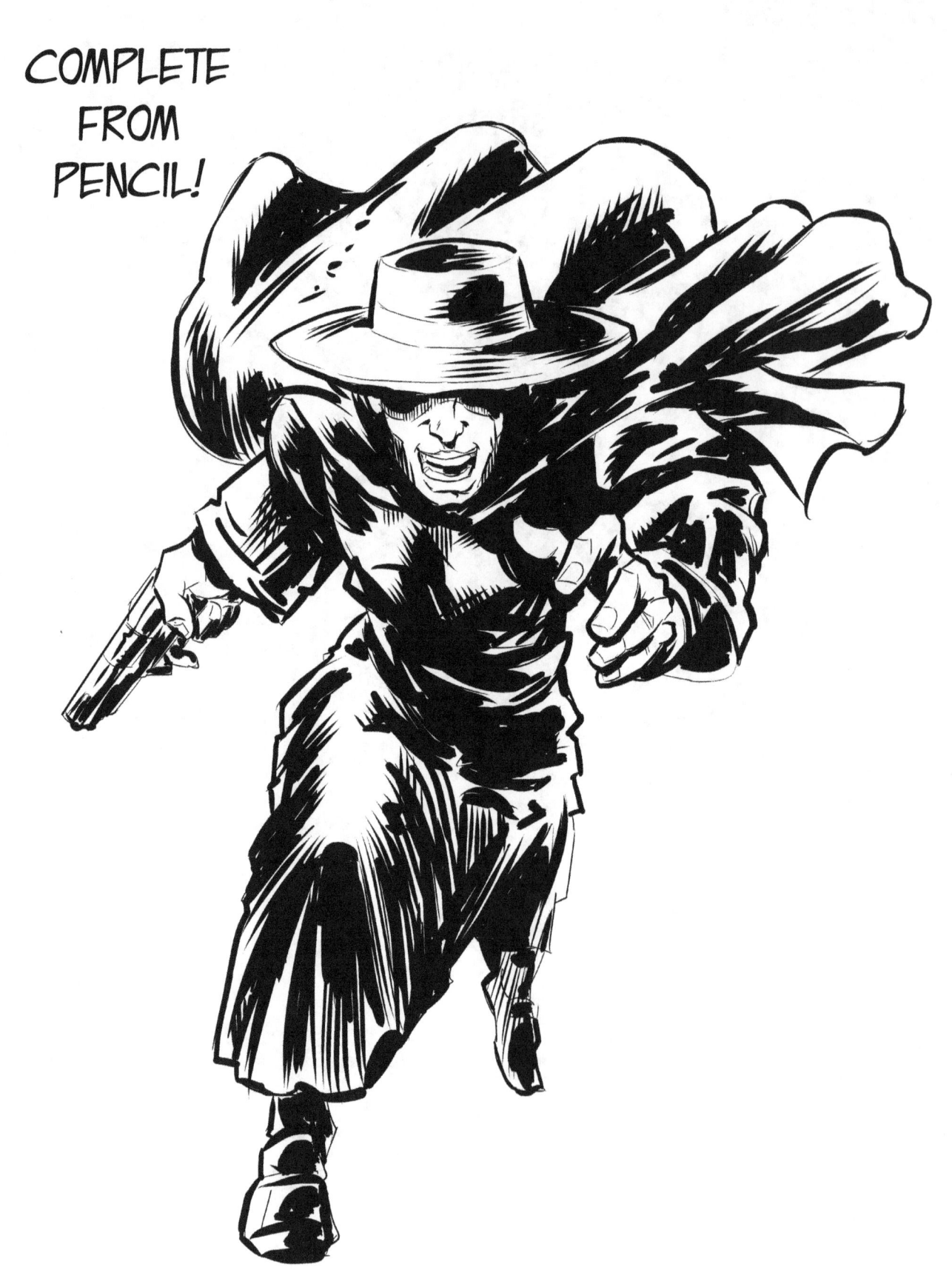

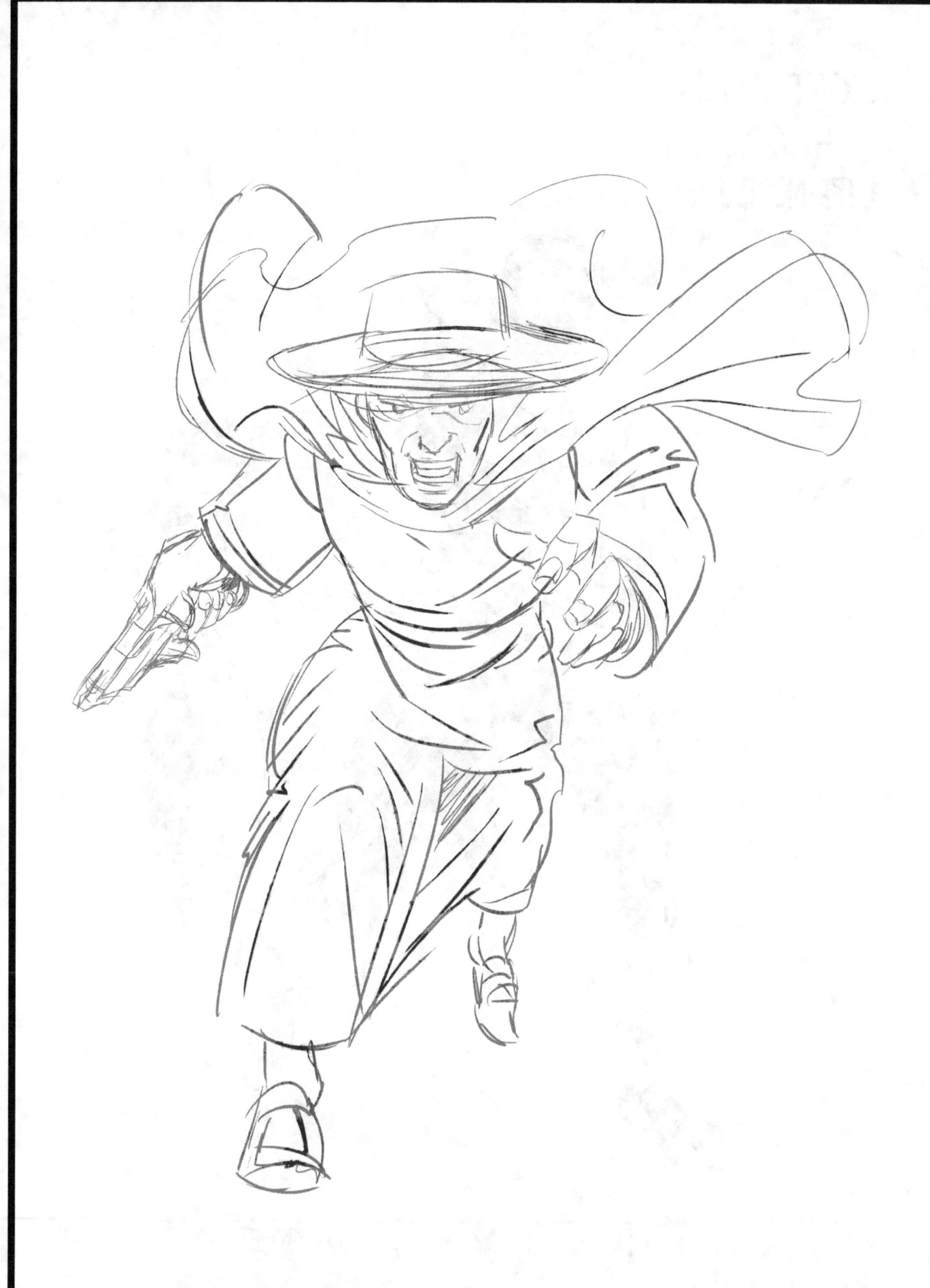

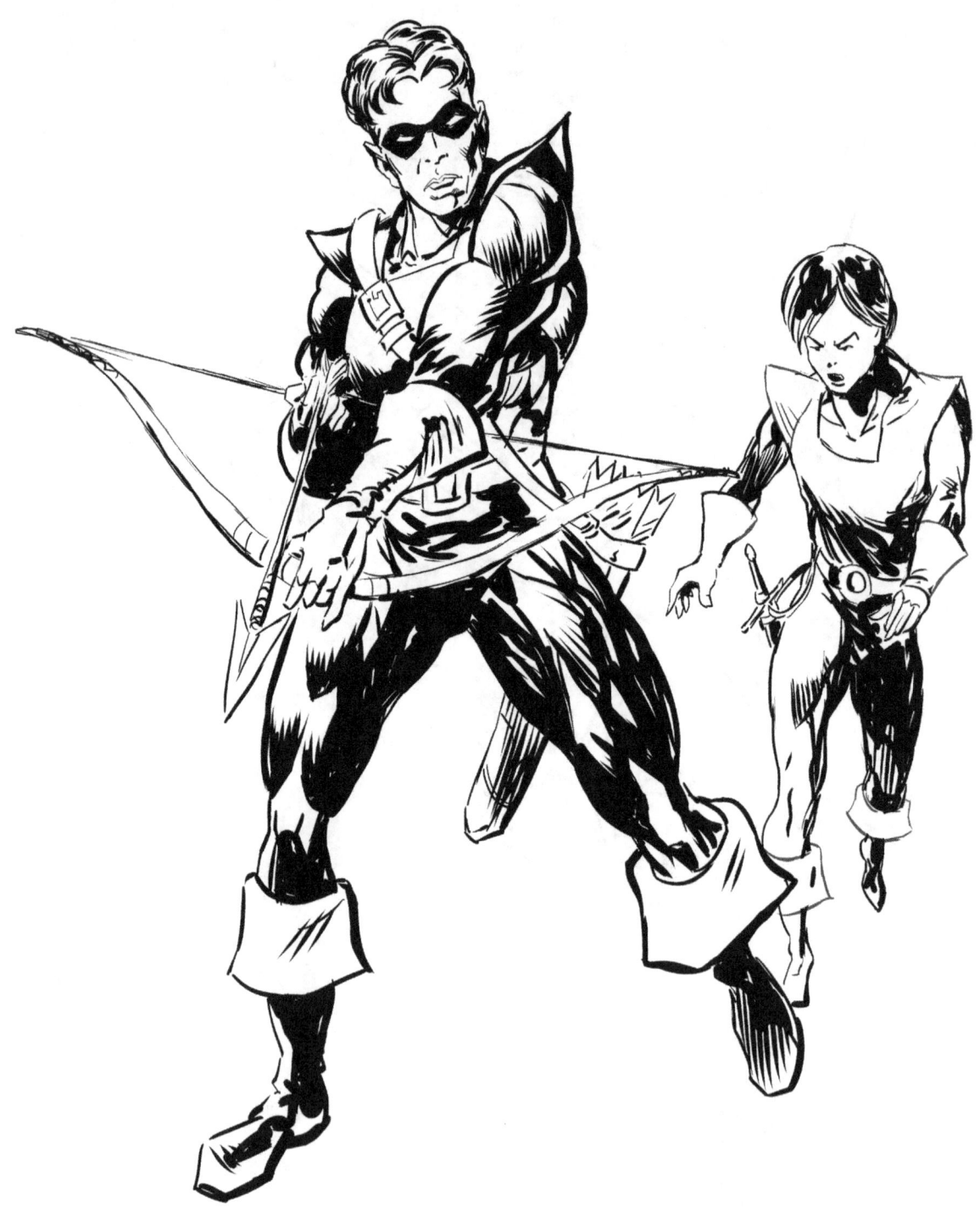

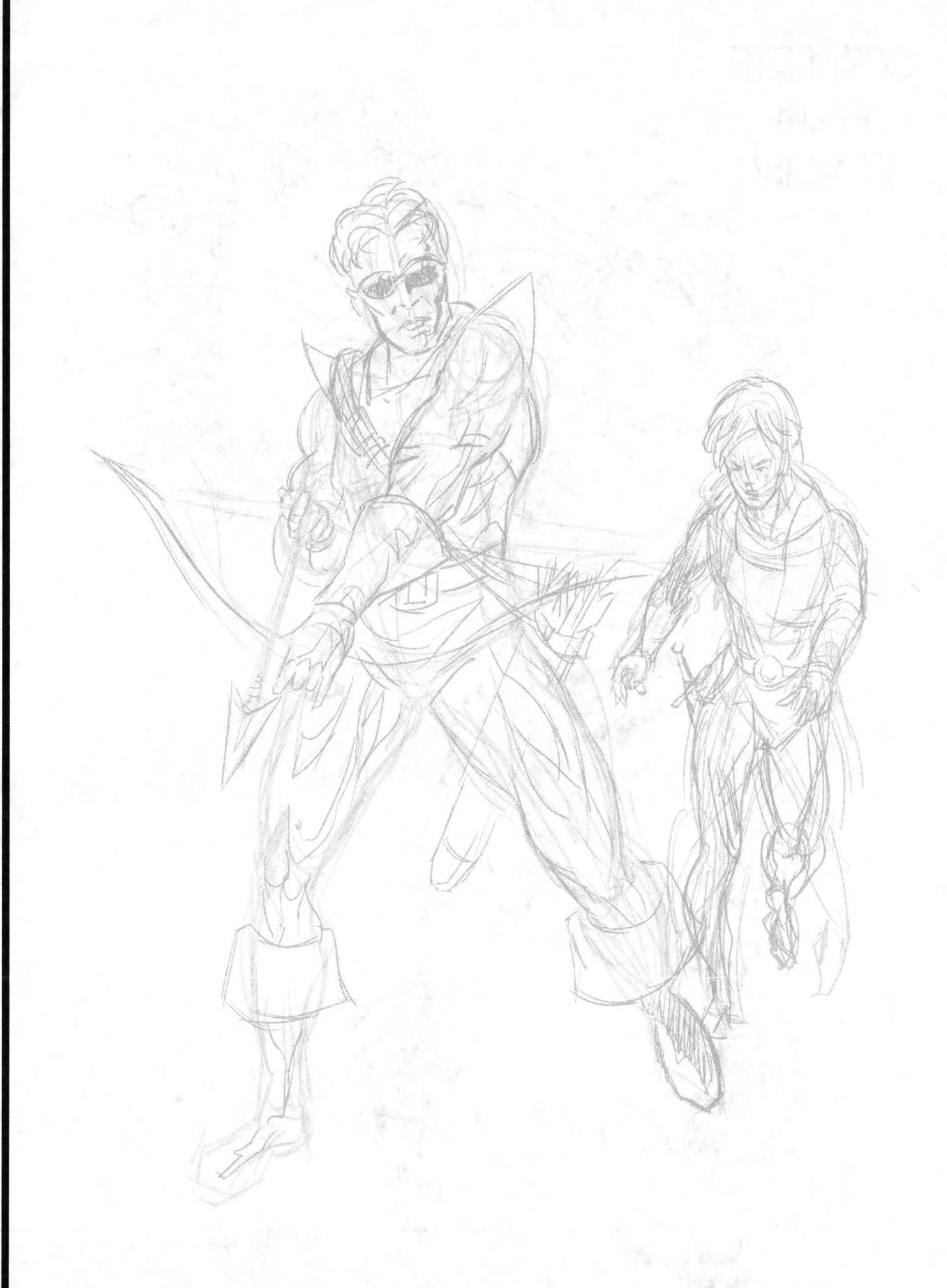

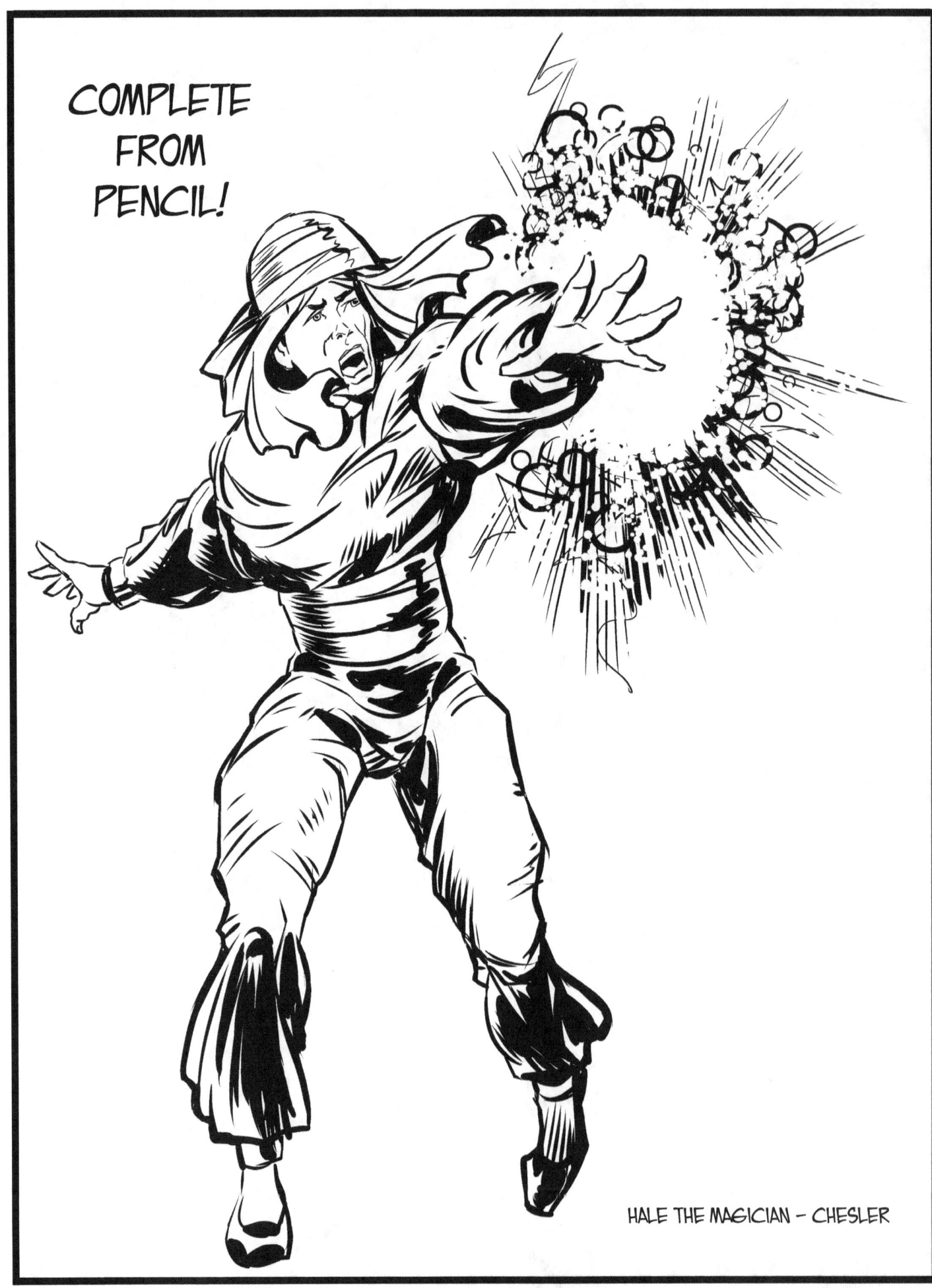

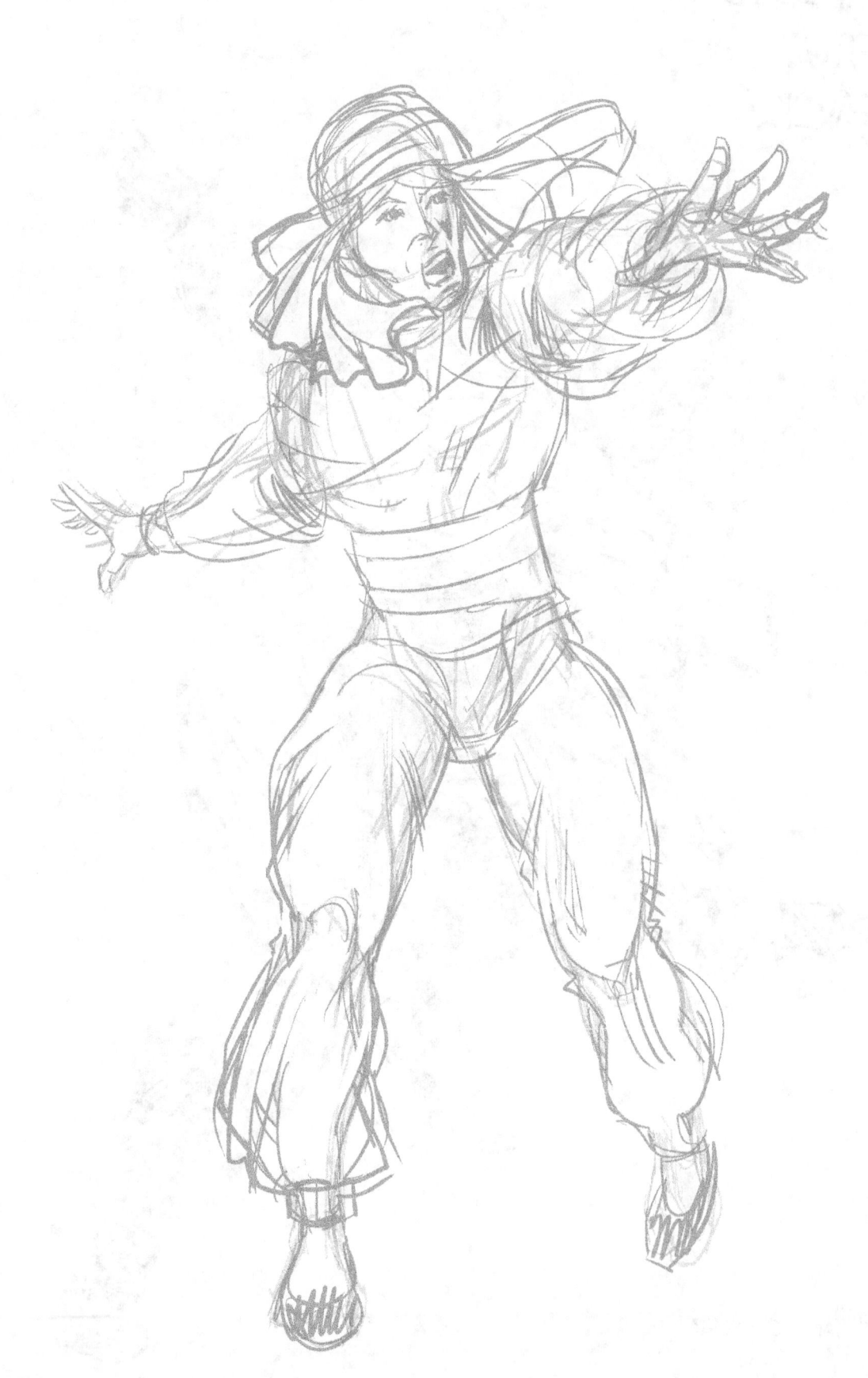

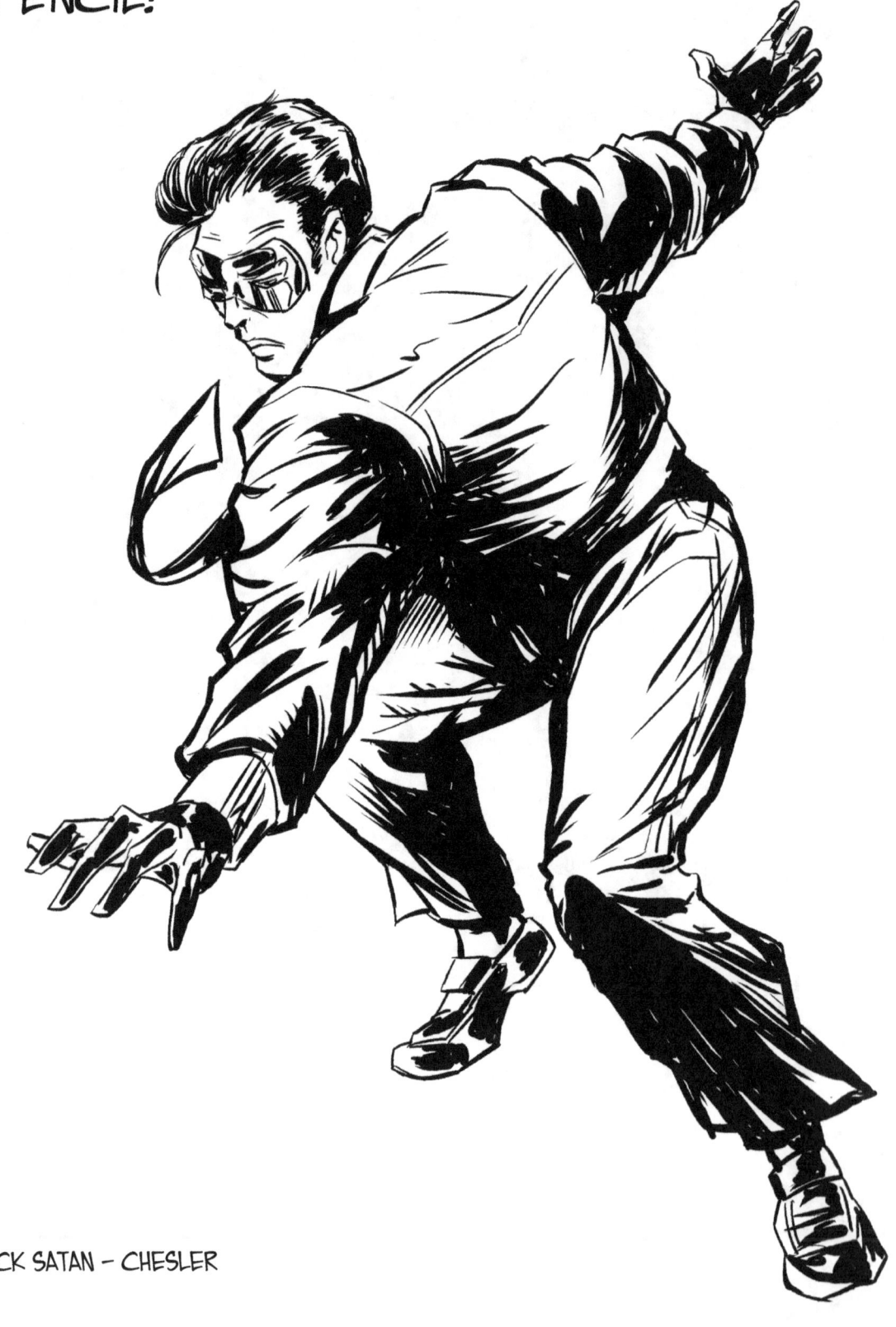

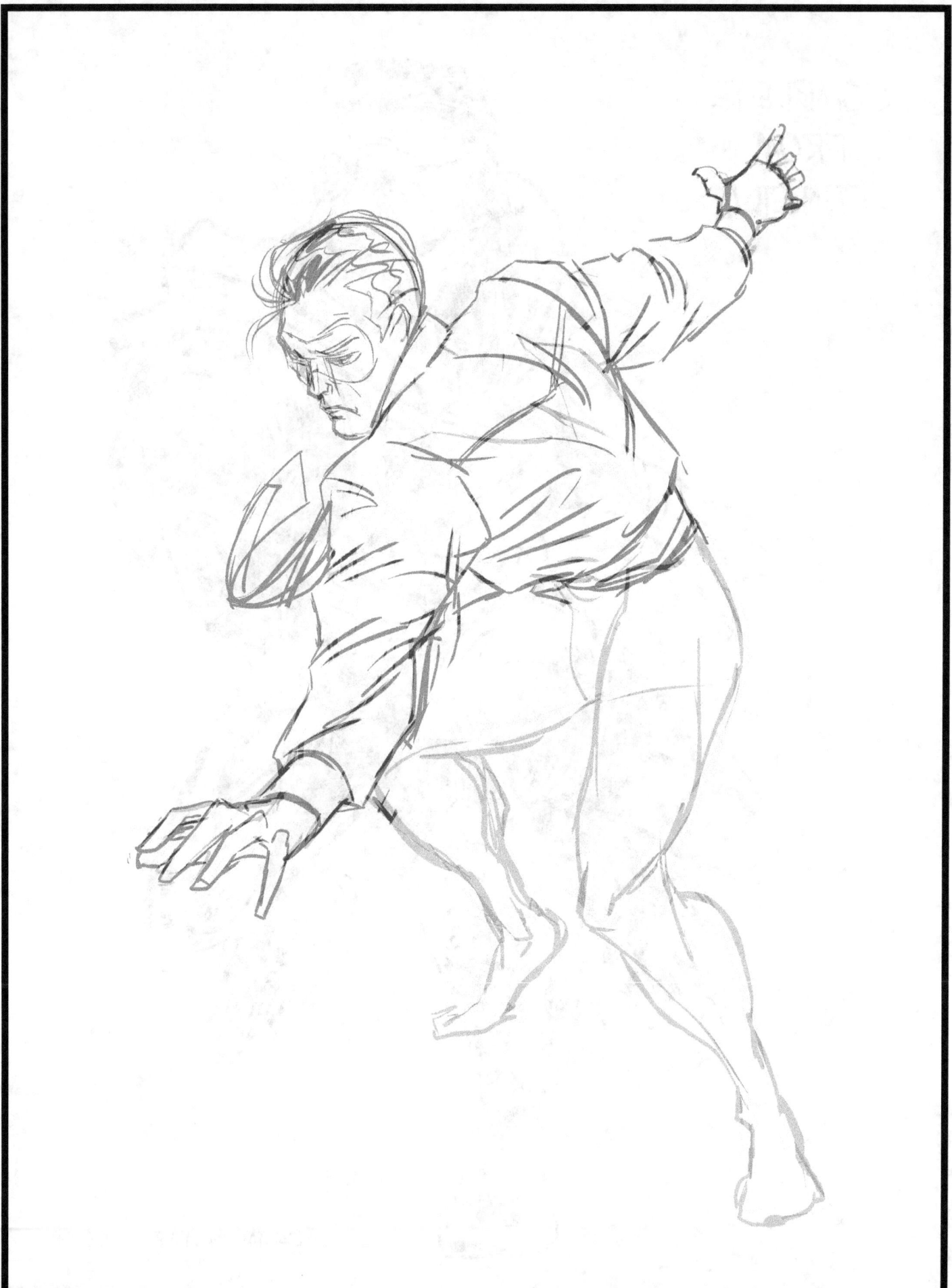

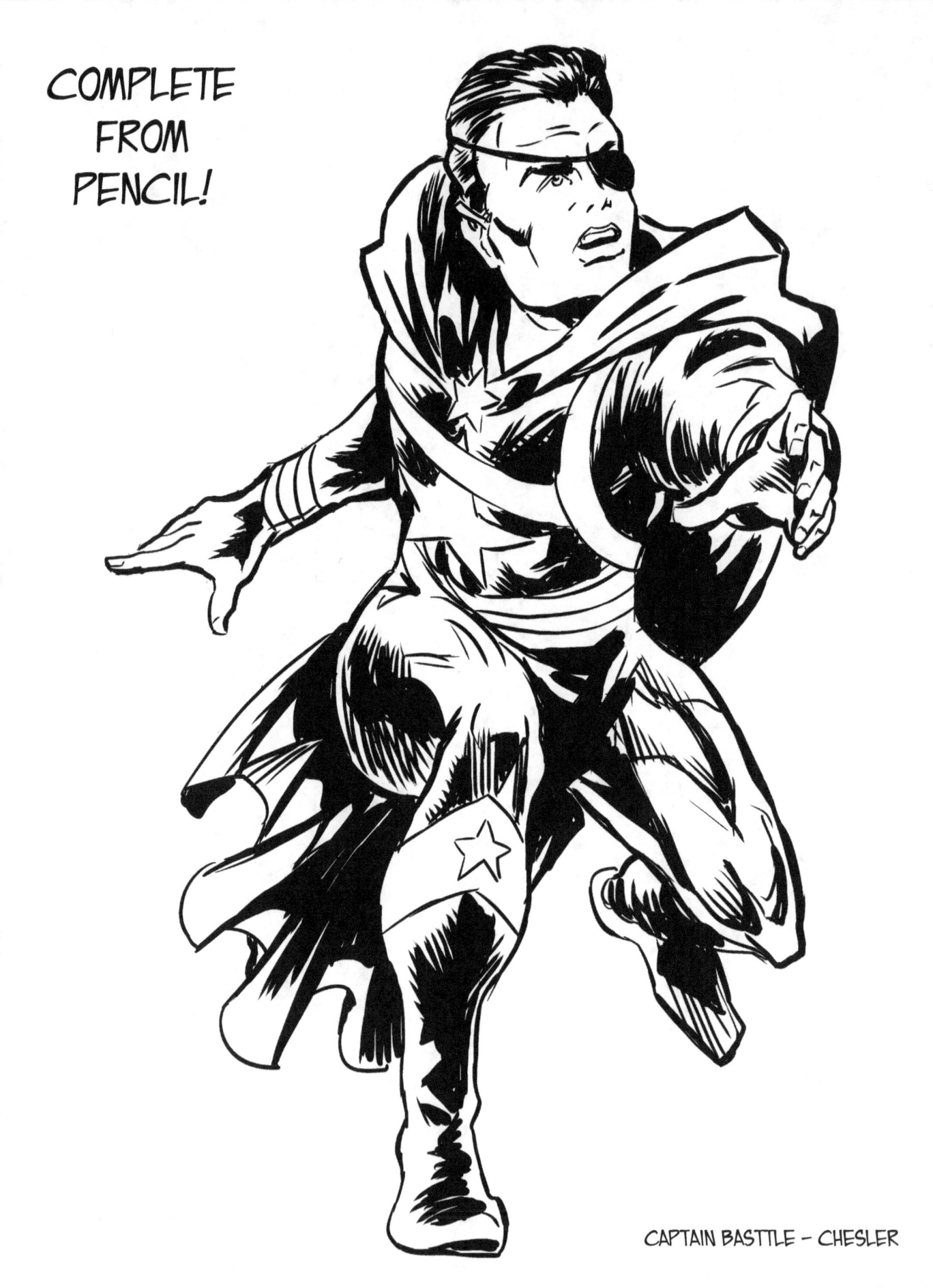

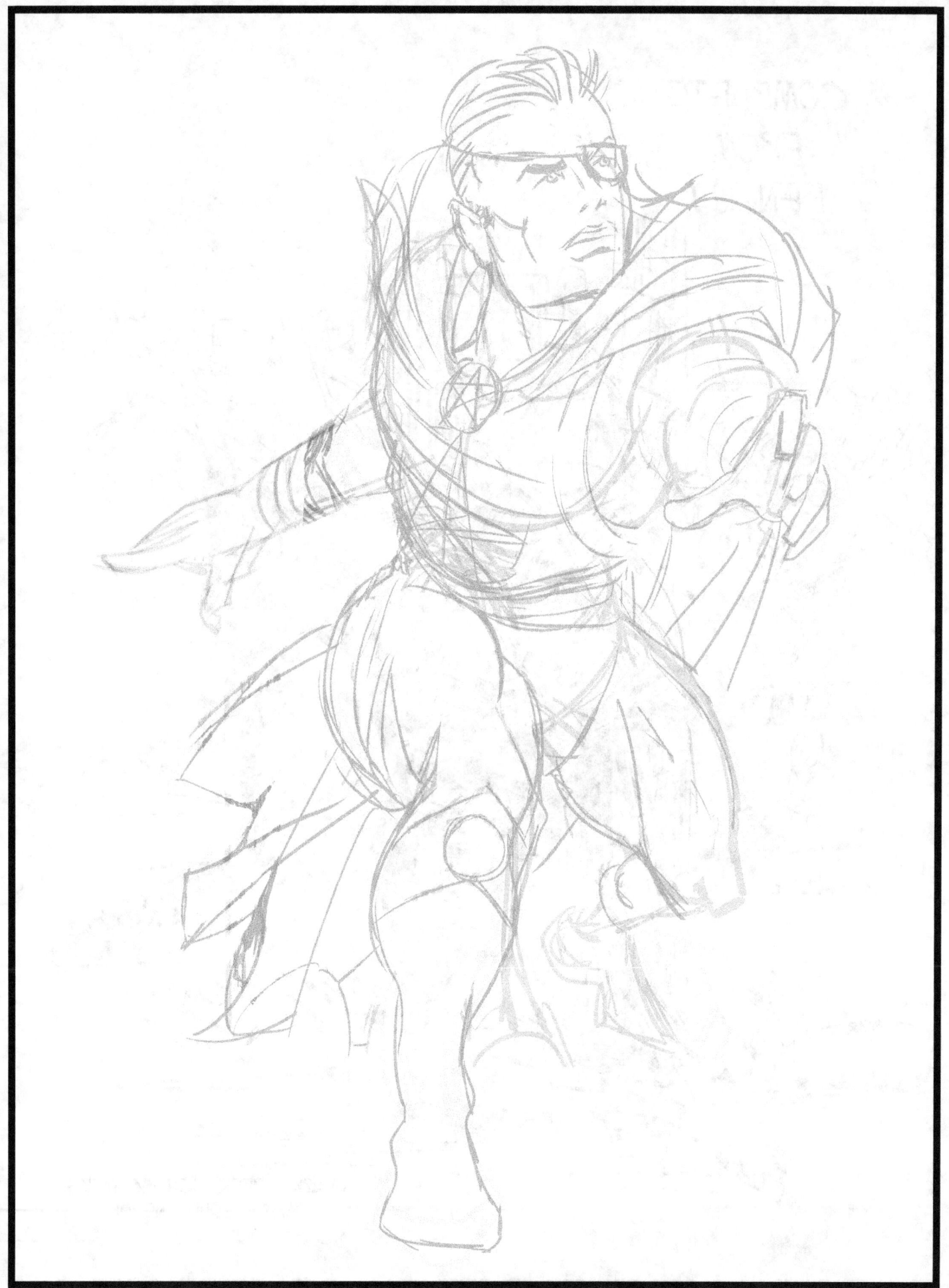

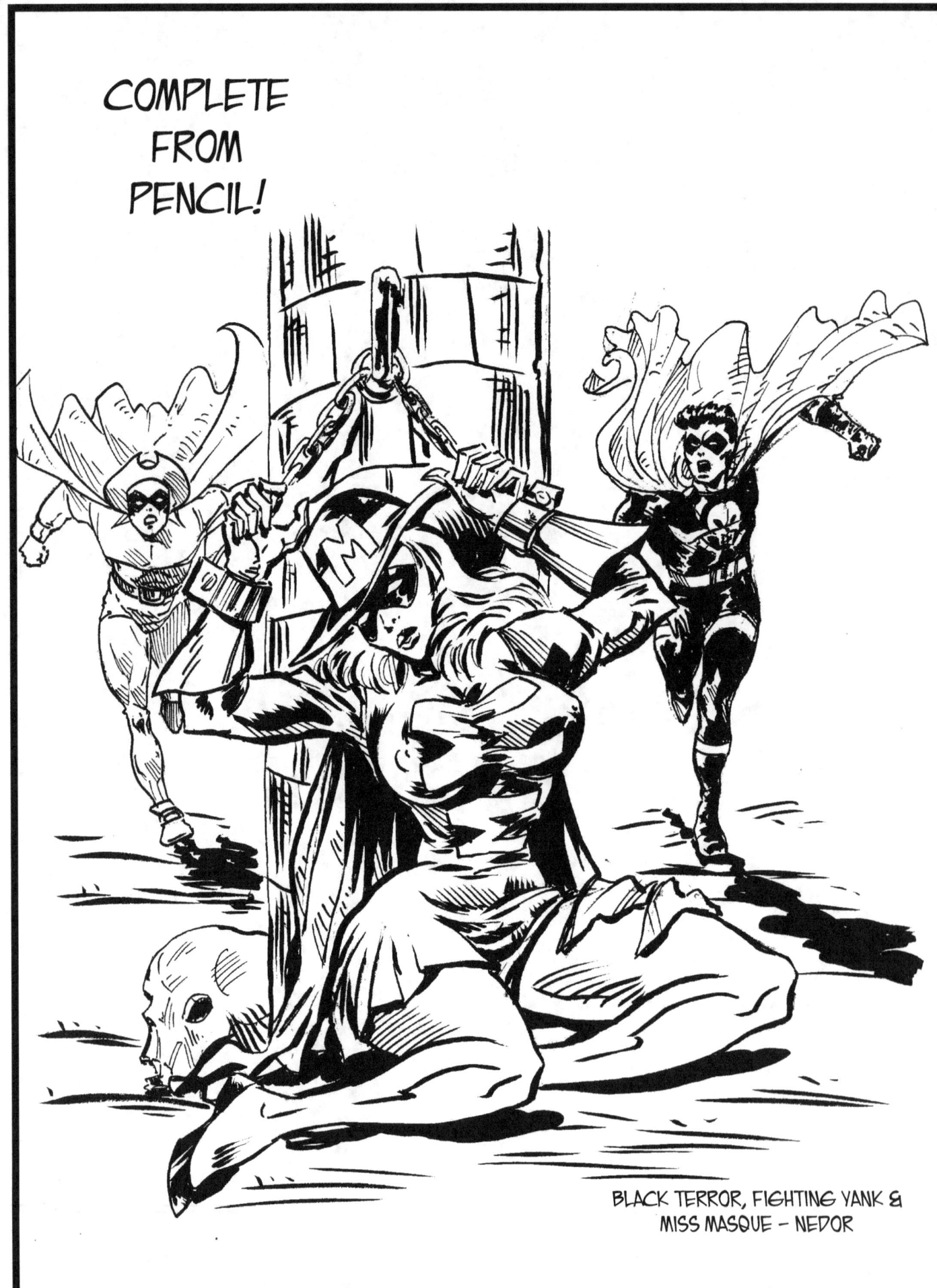

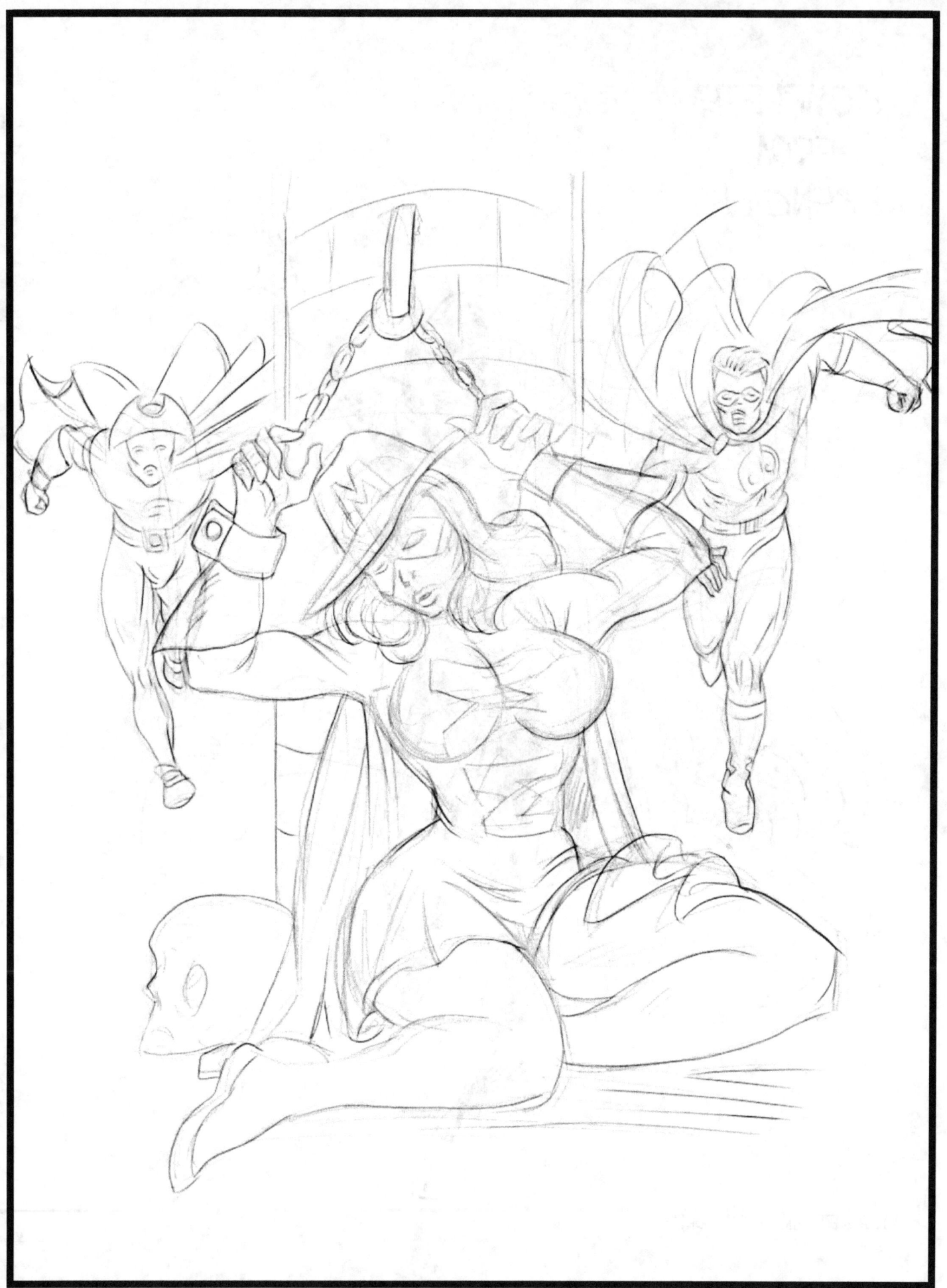

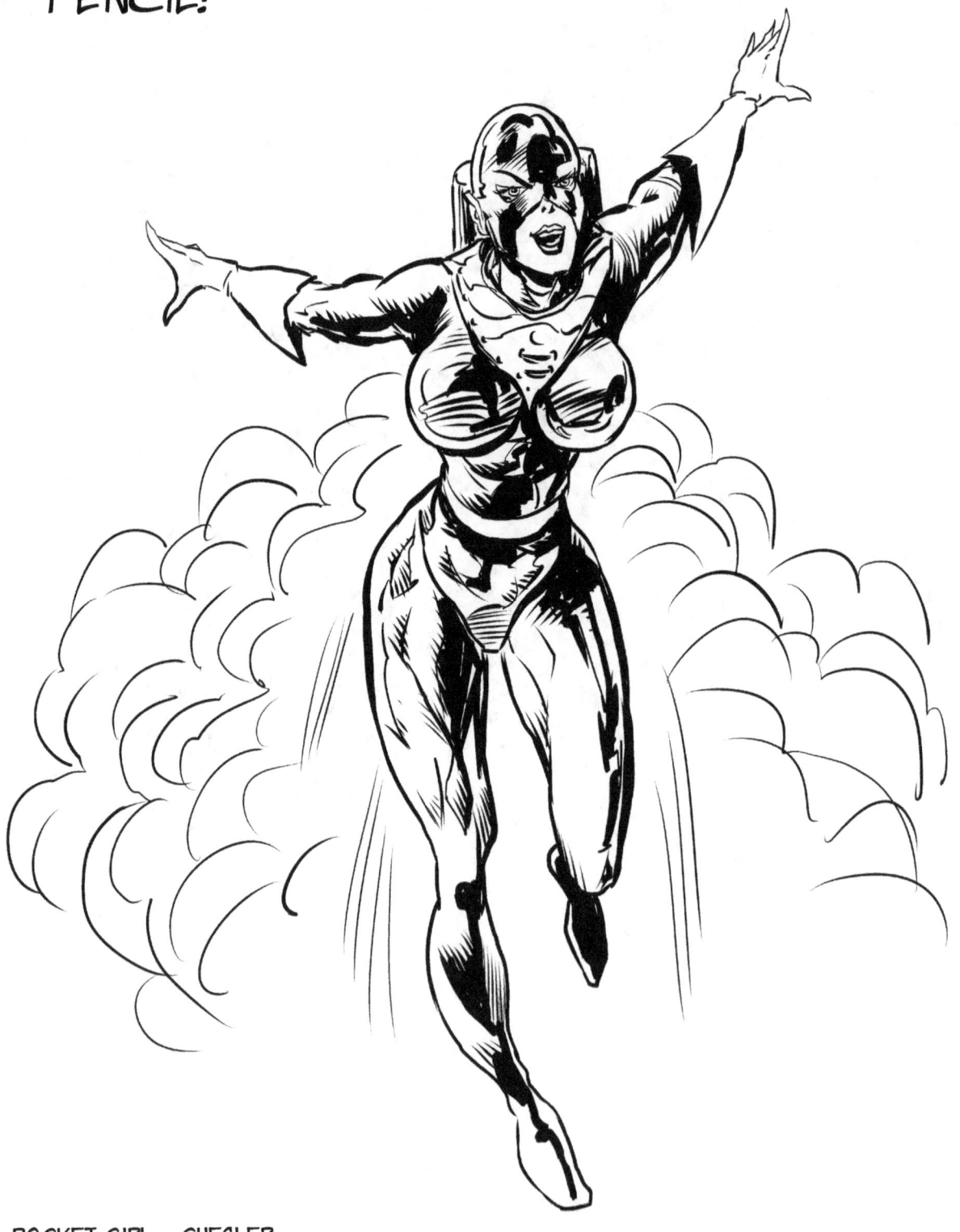

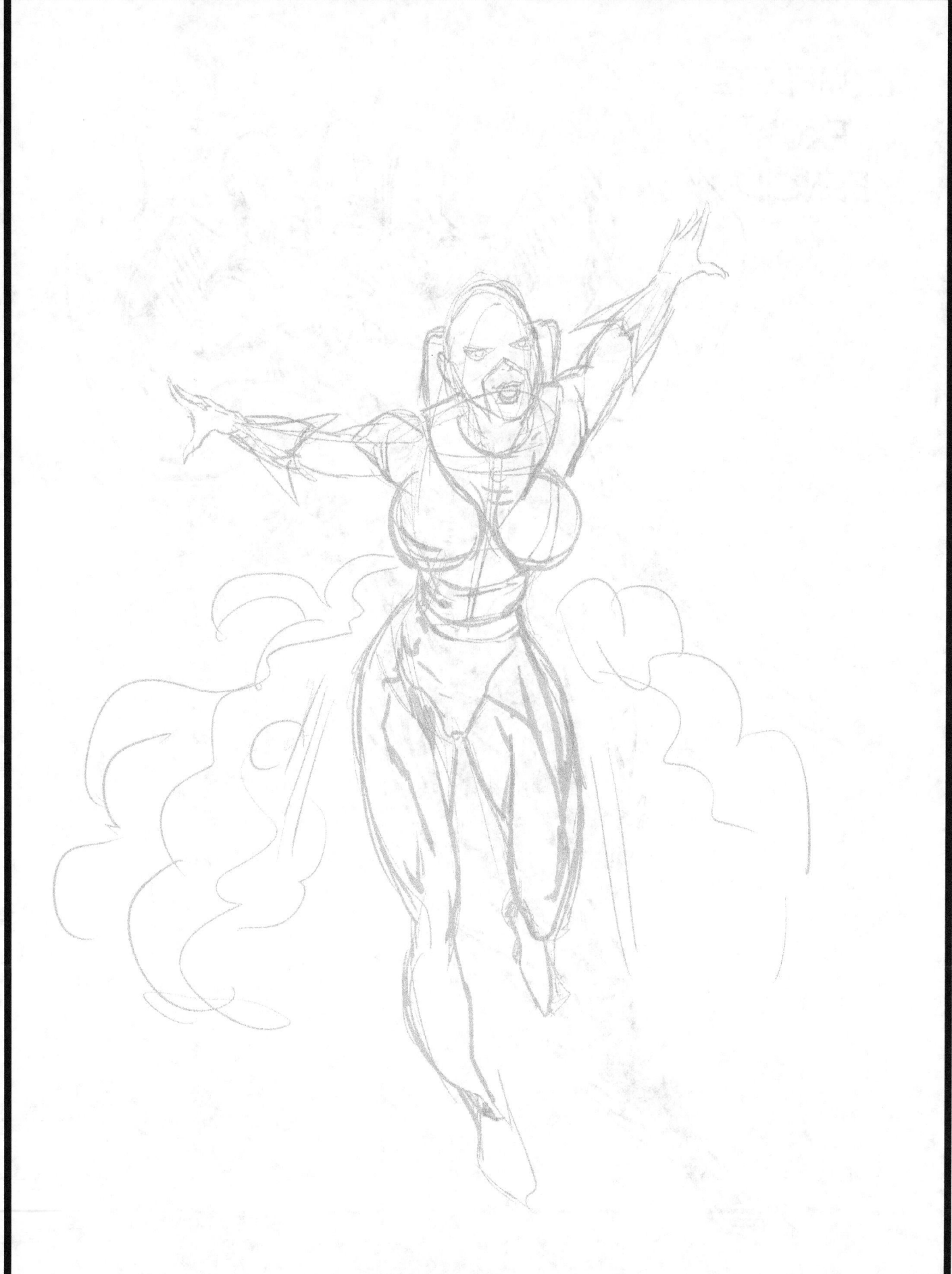

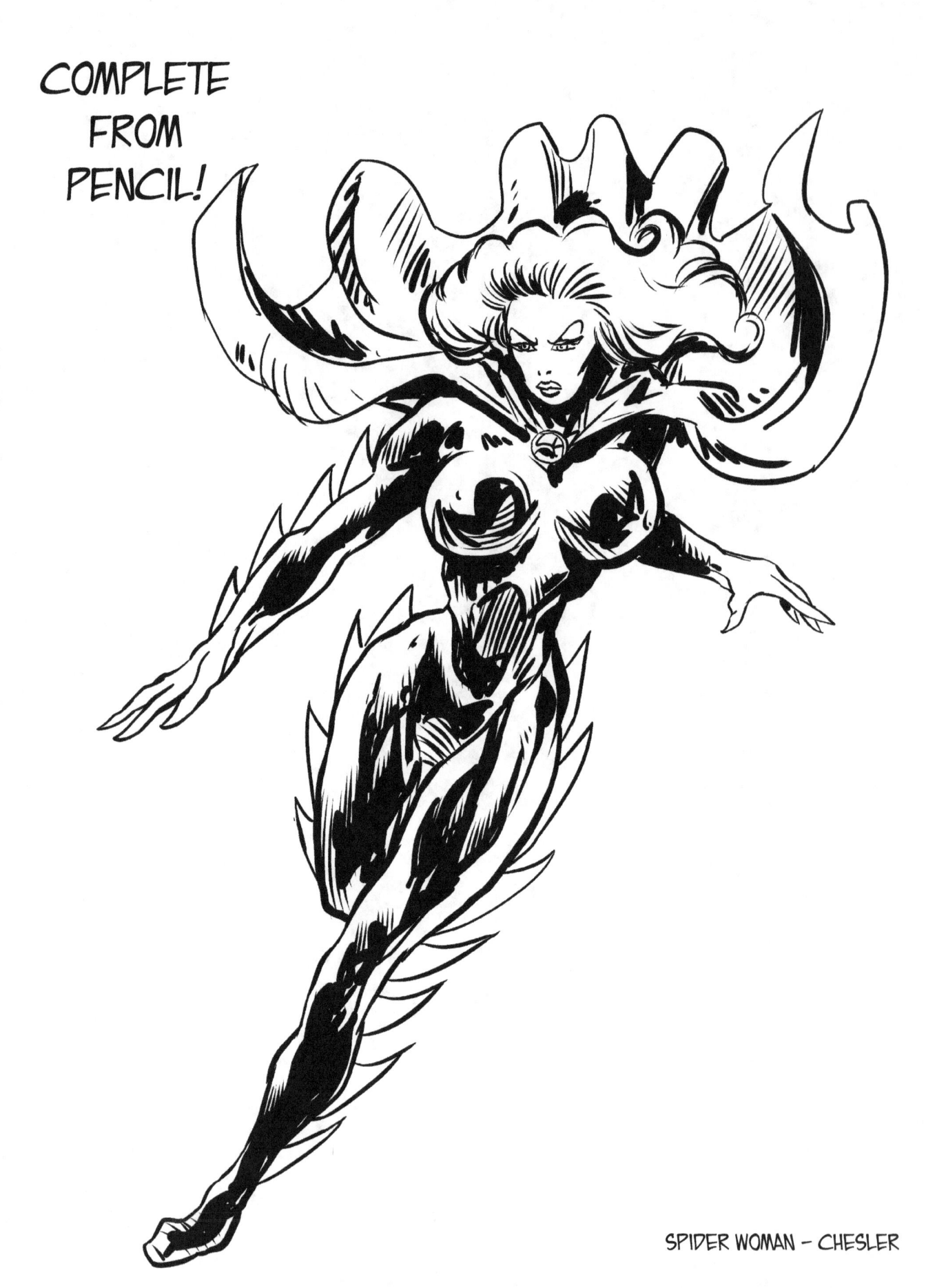

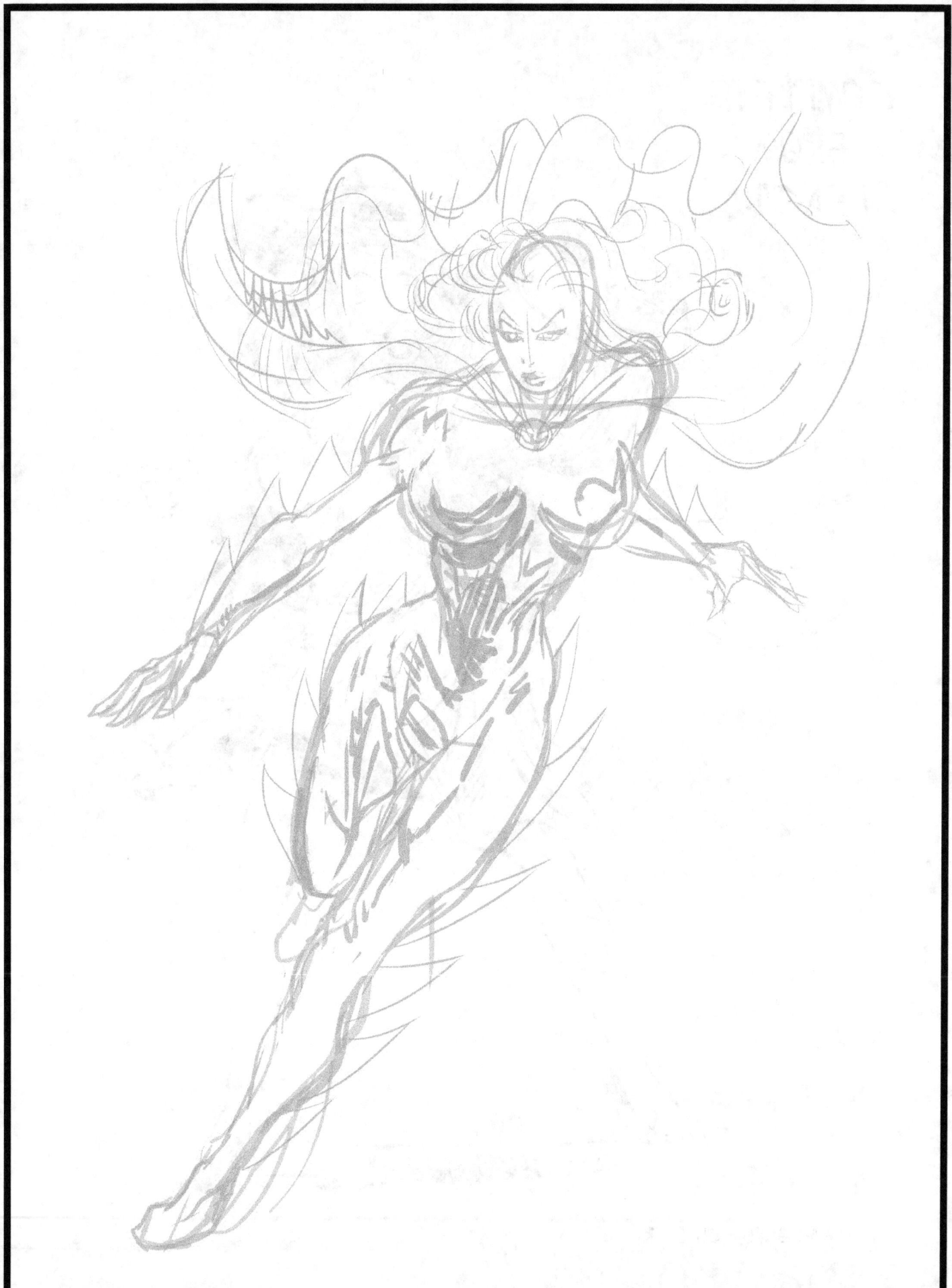

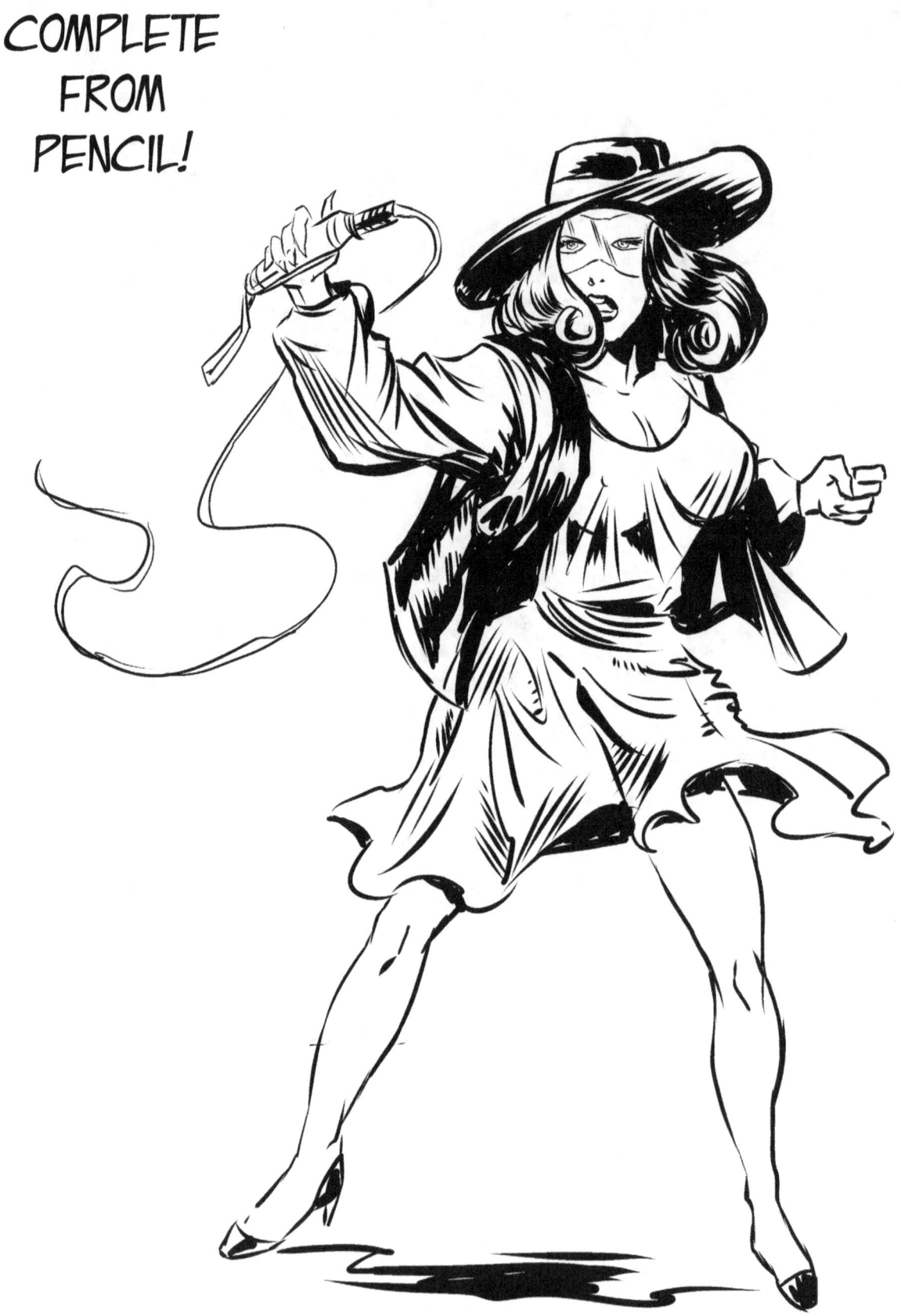

COMPLETE FROM PENCIL!

VEILED AVENGERS - CHESLER

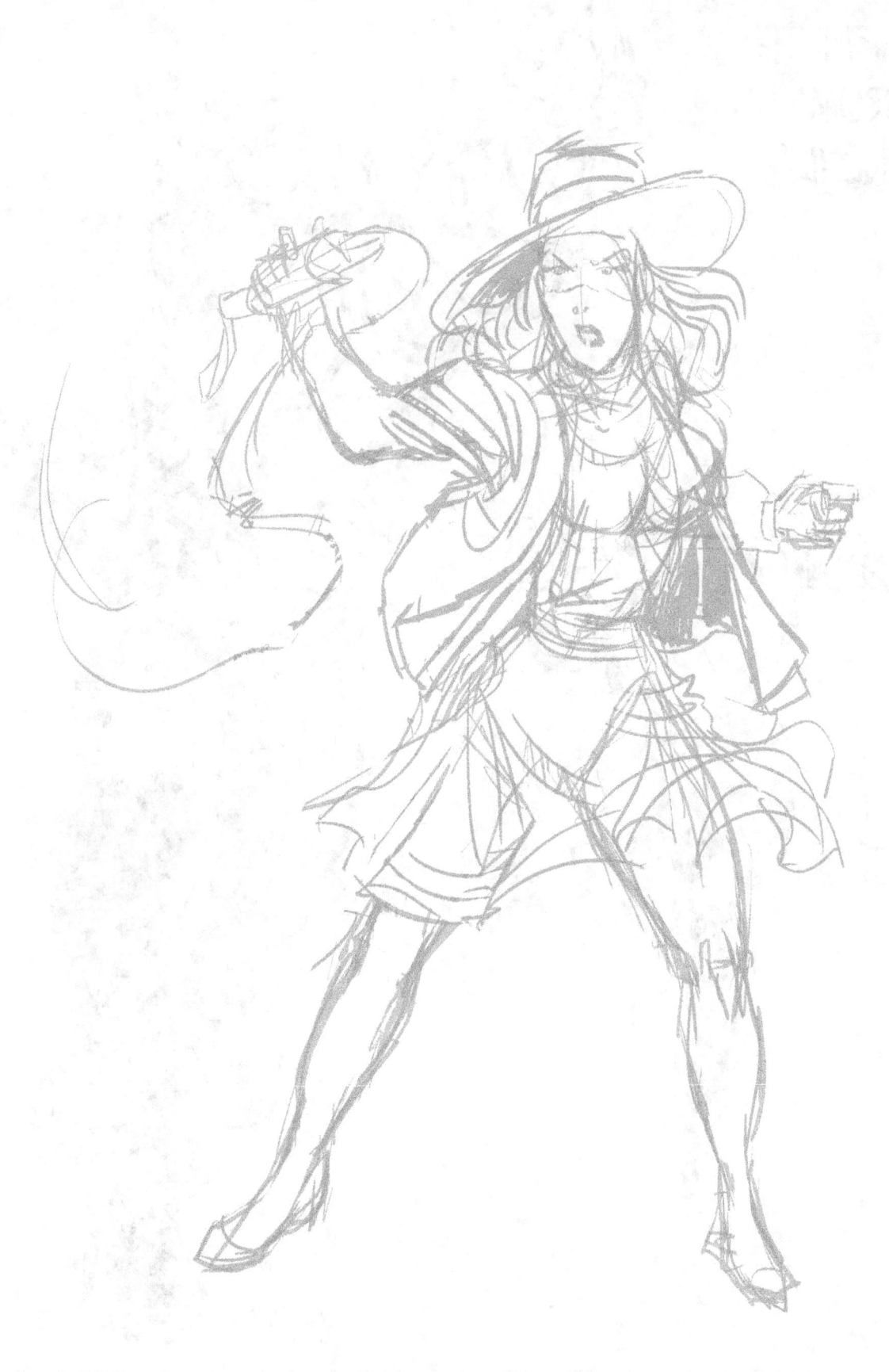

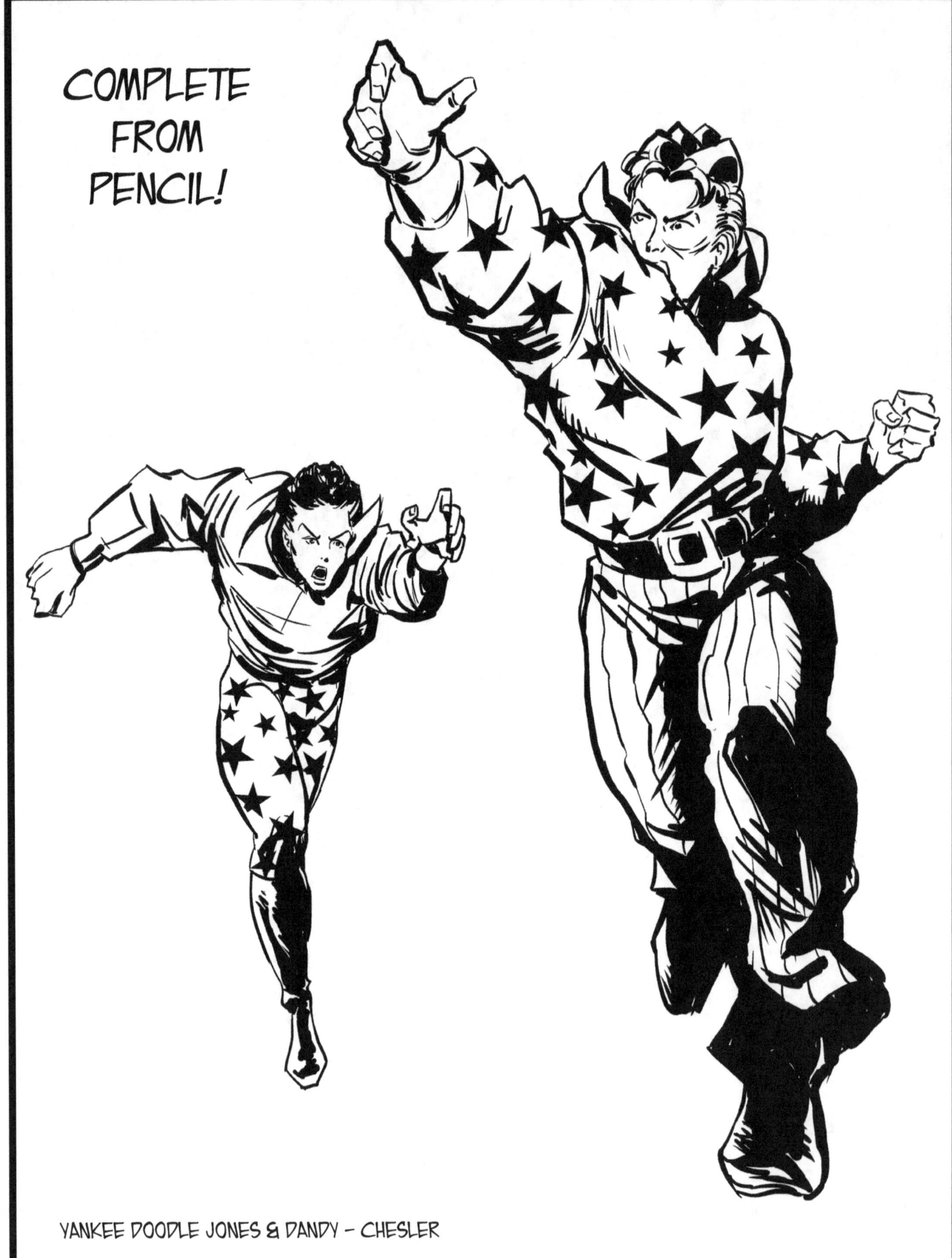

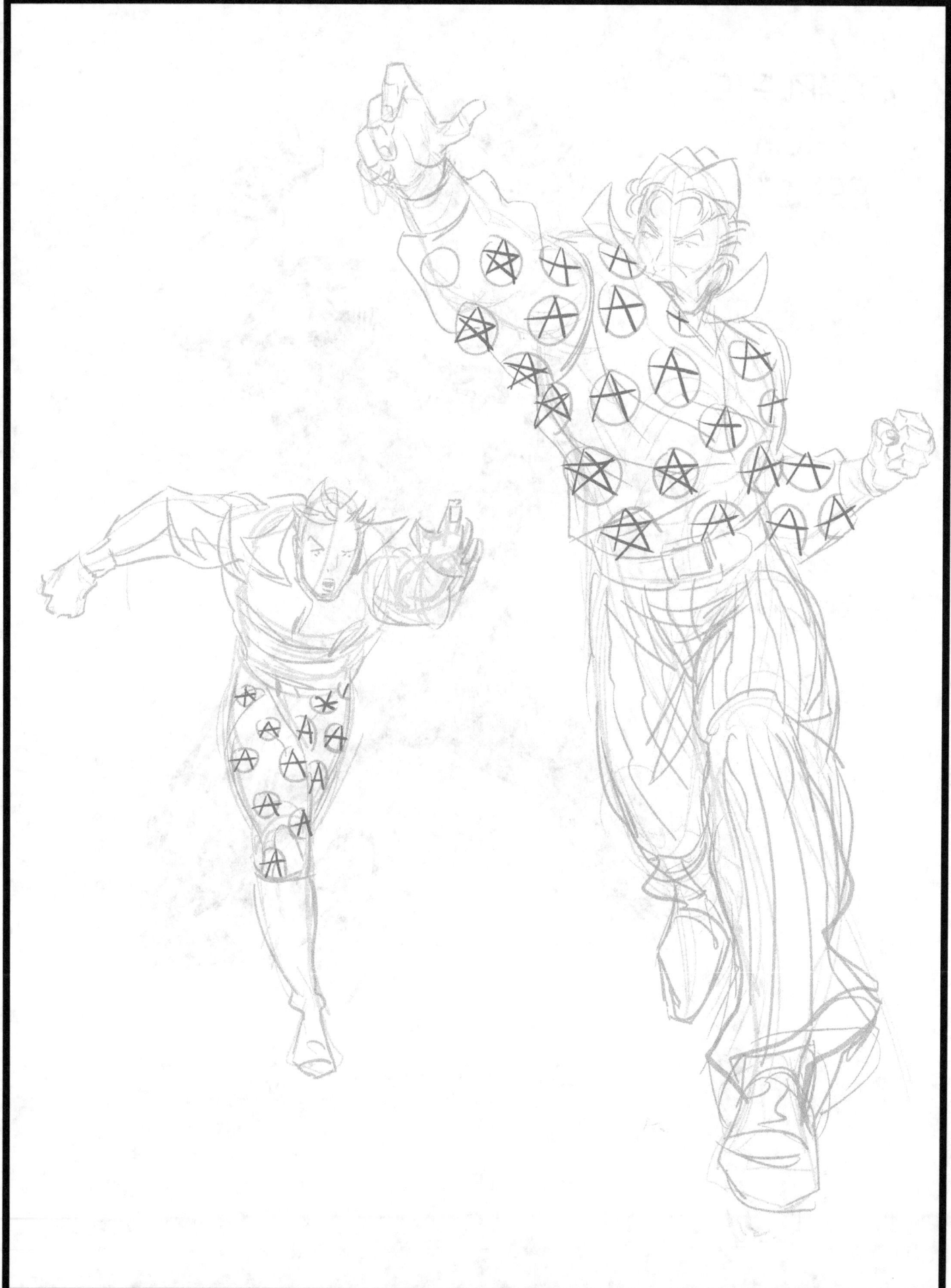

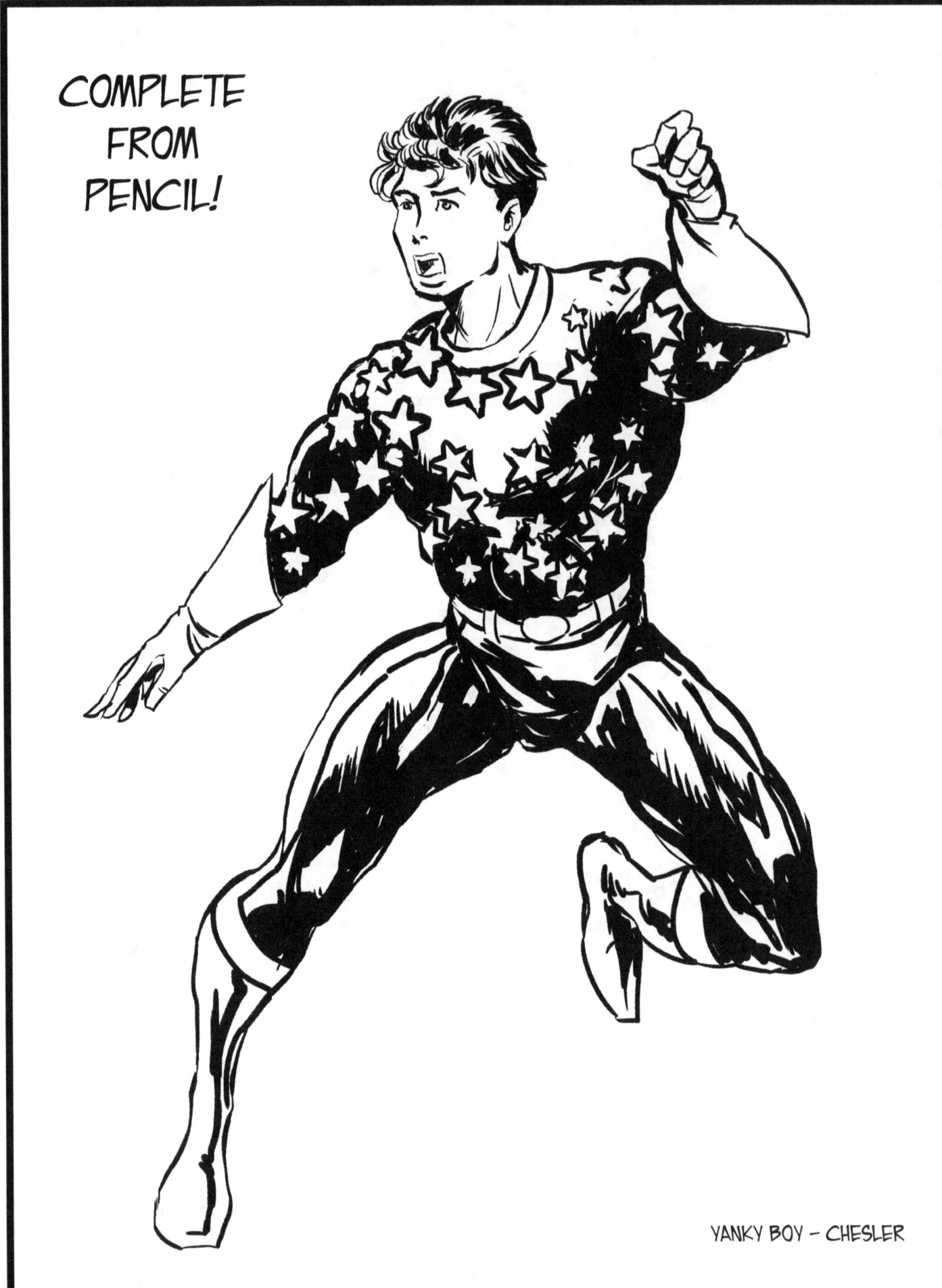

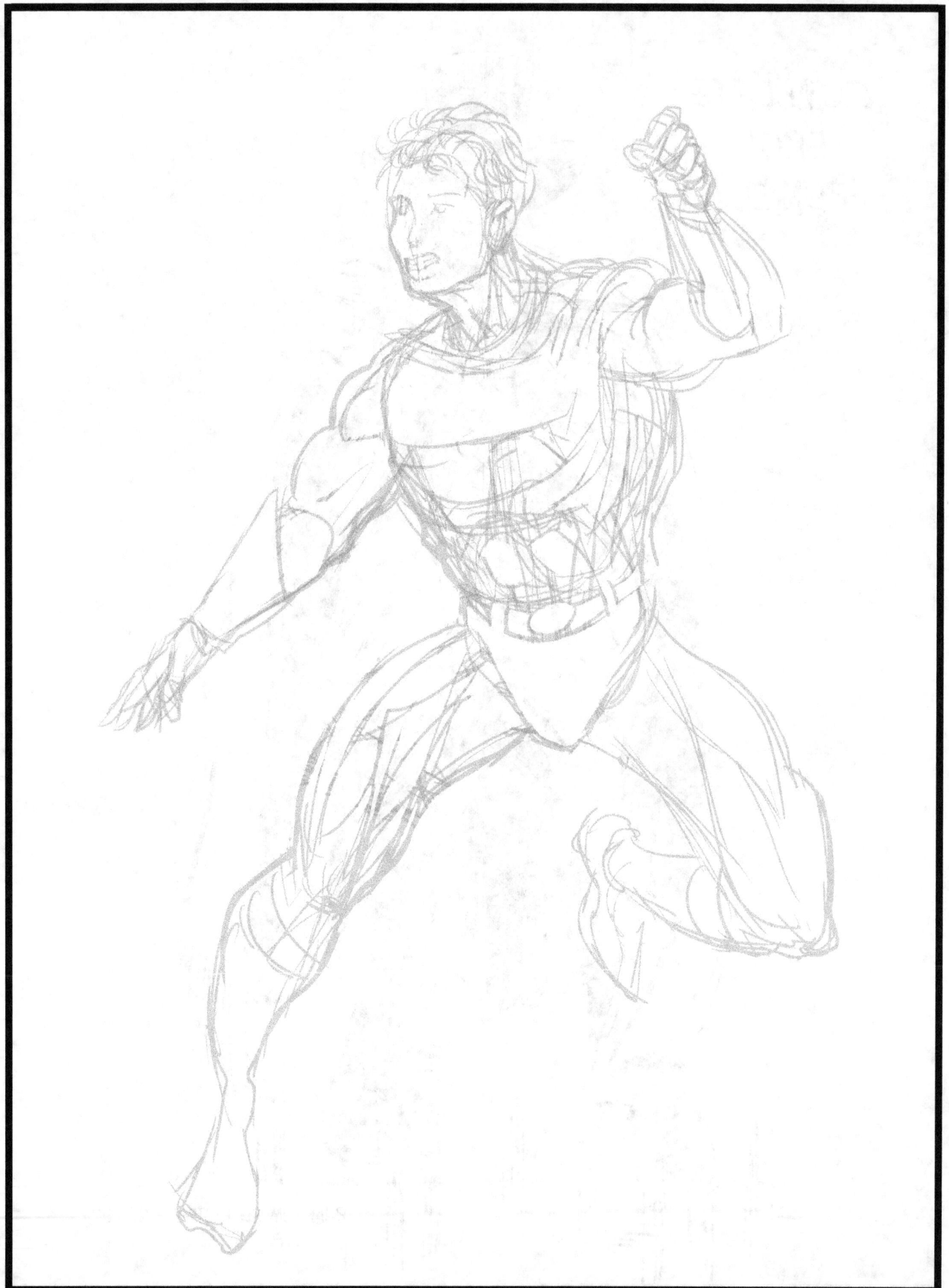

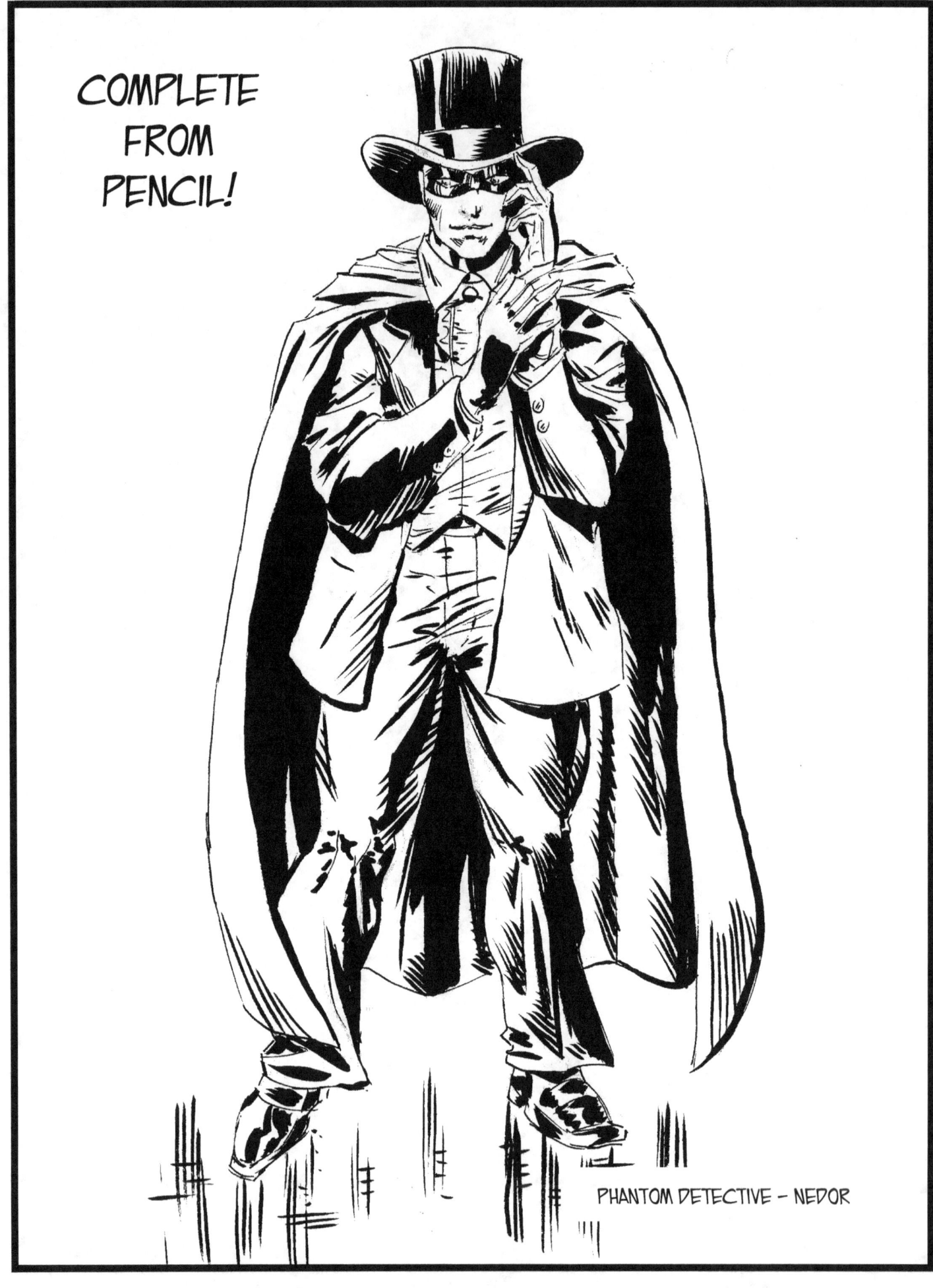

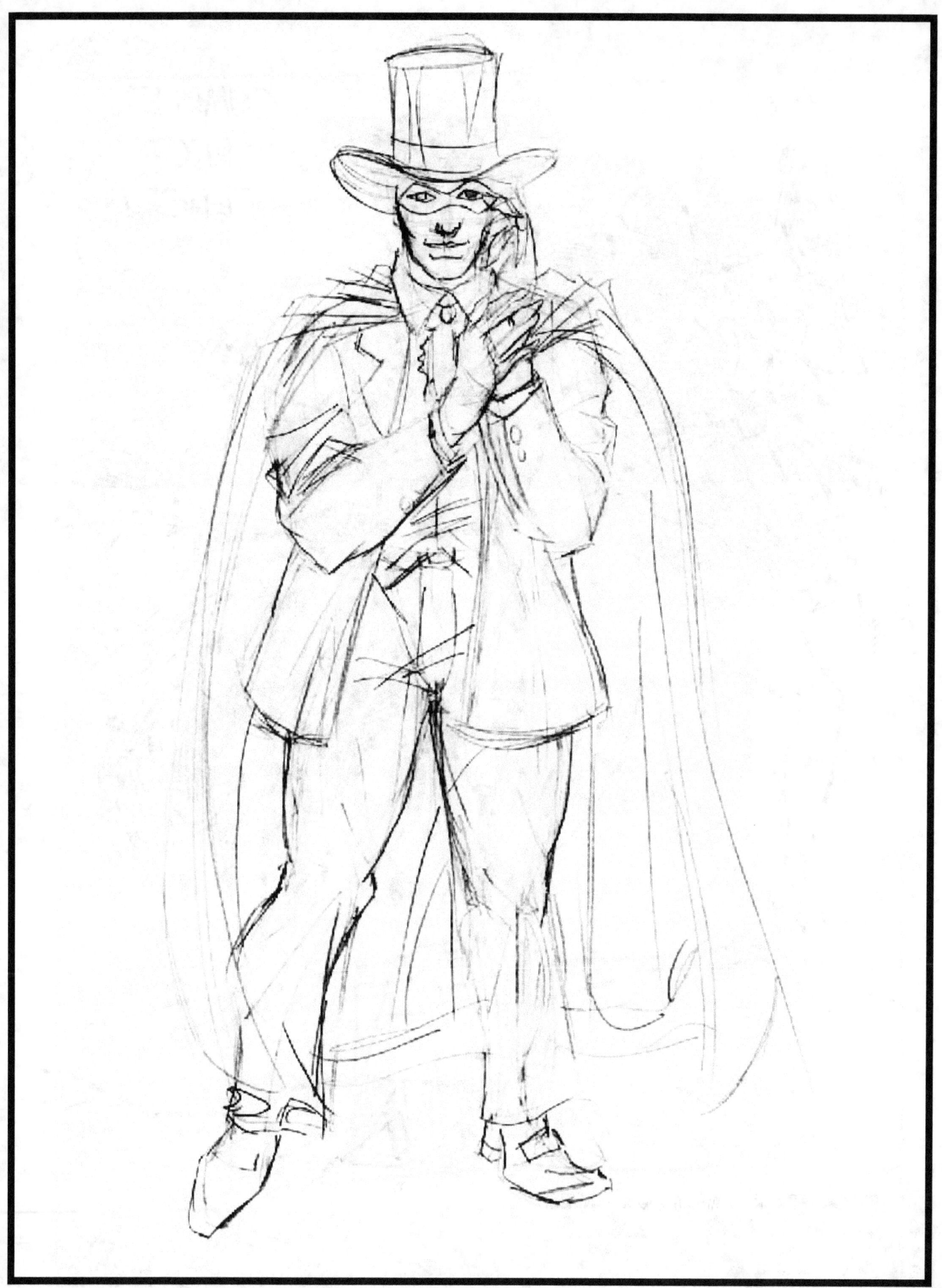

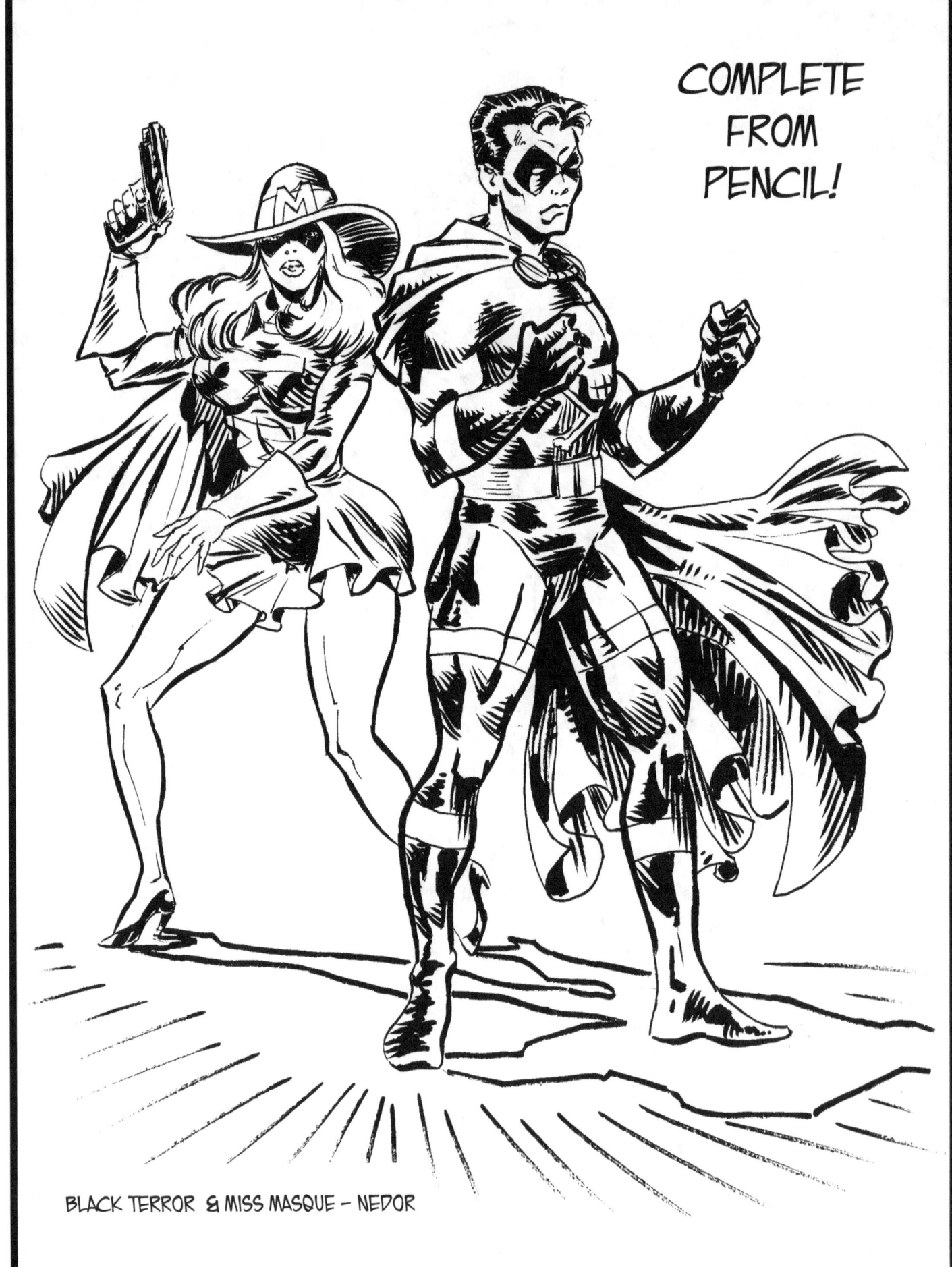

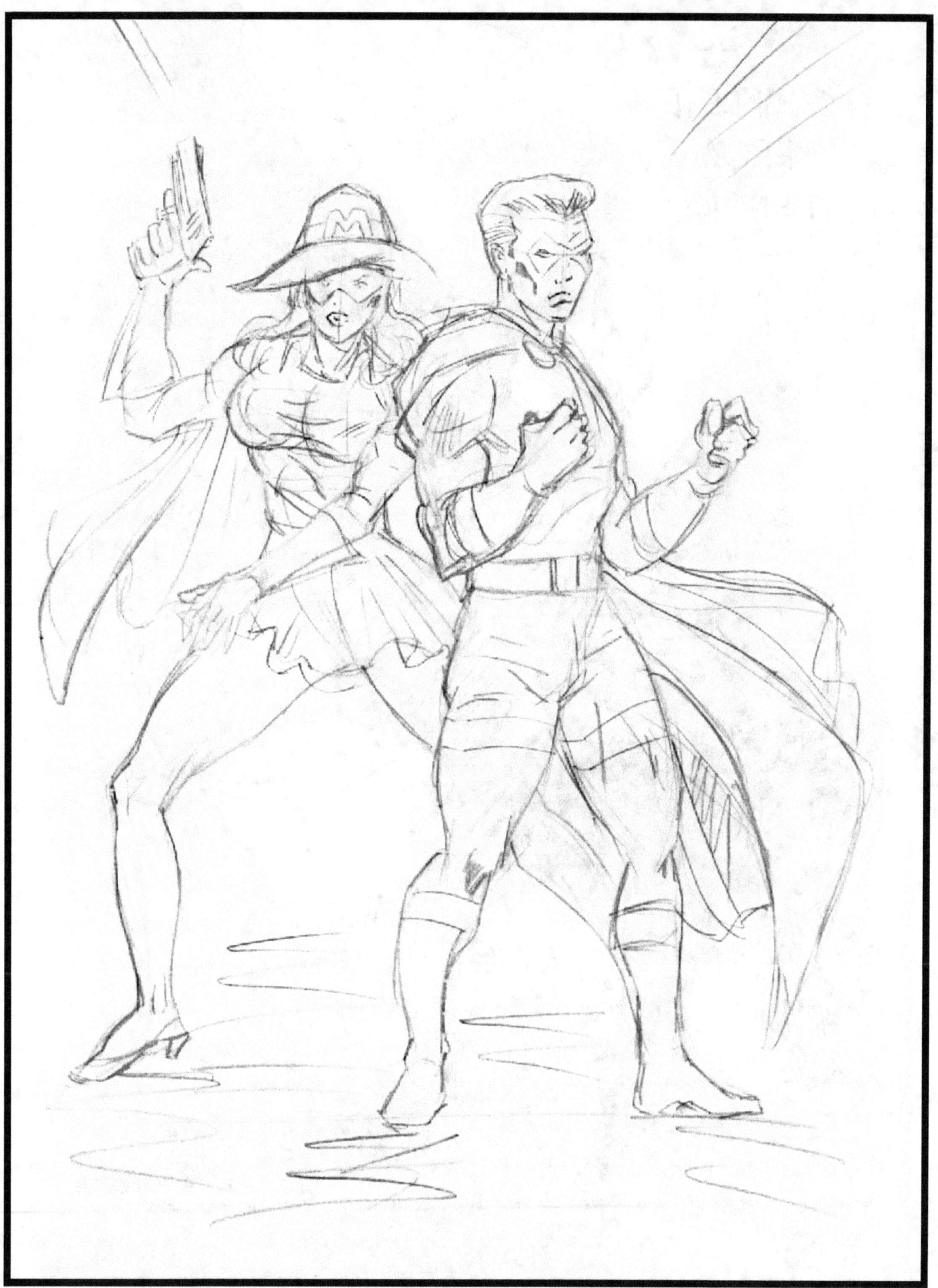

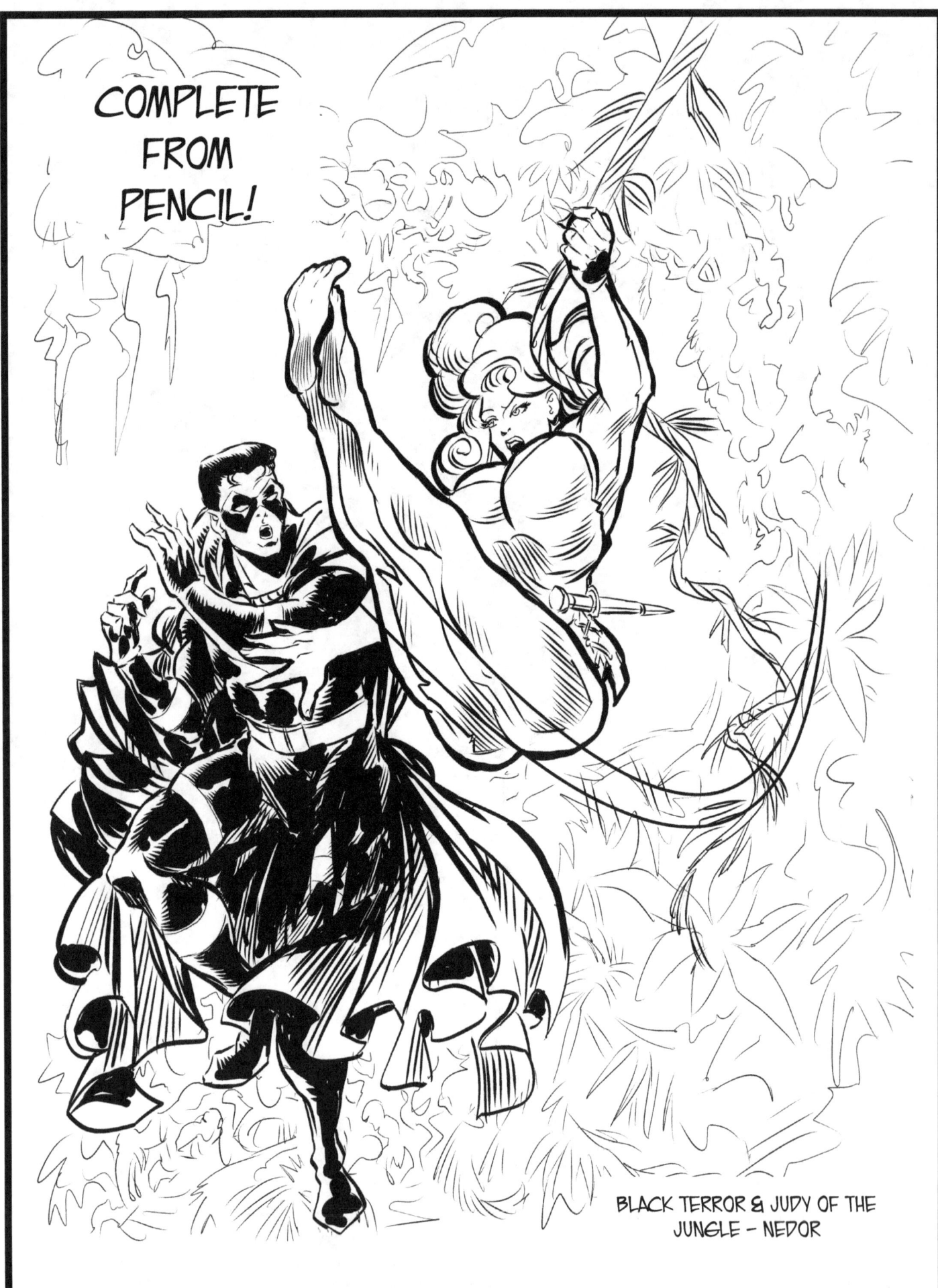

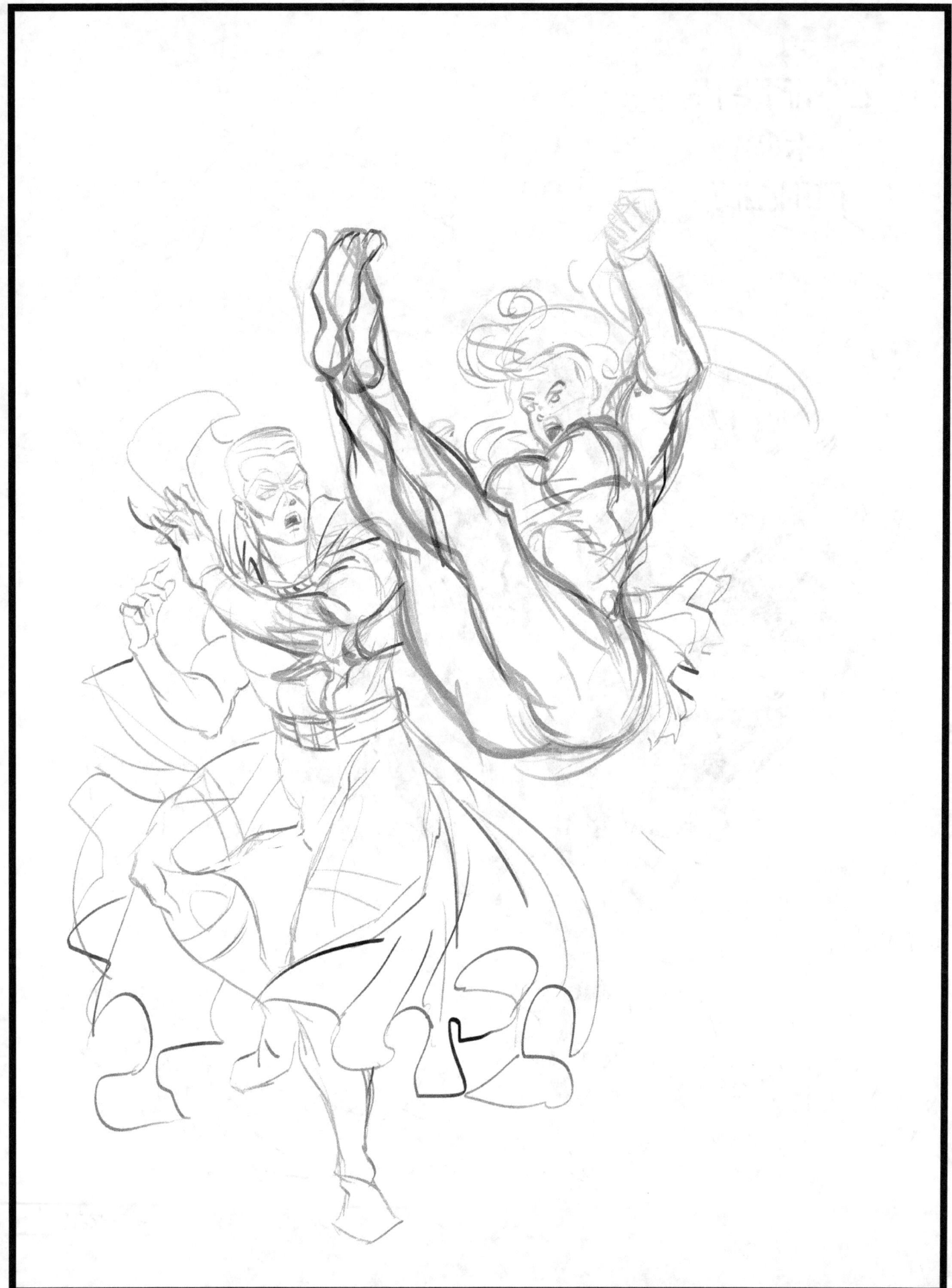

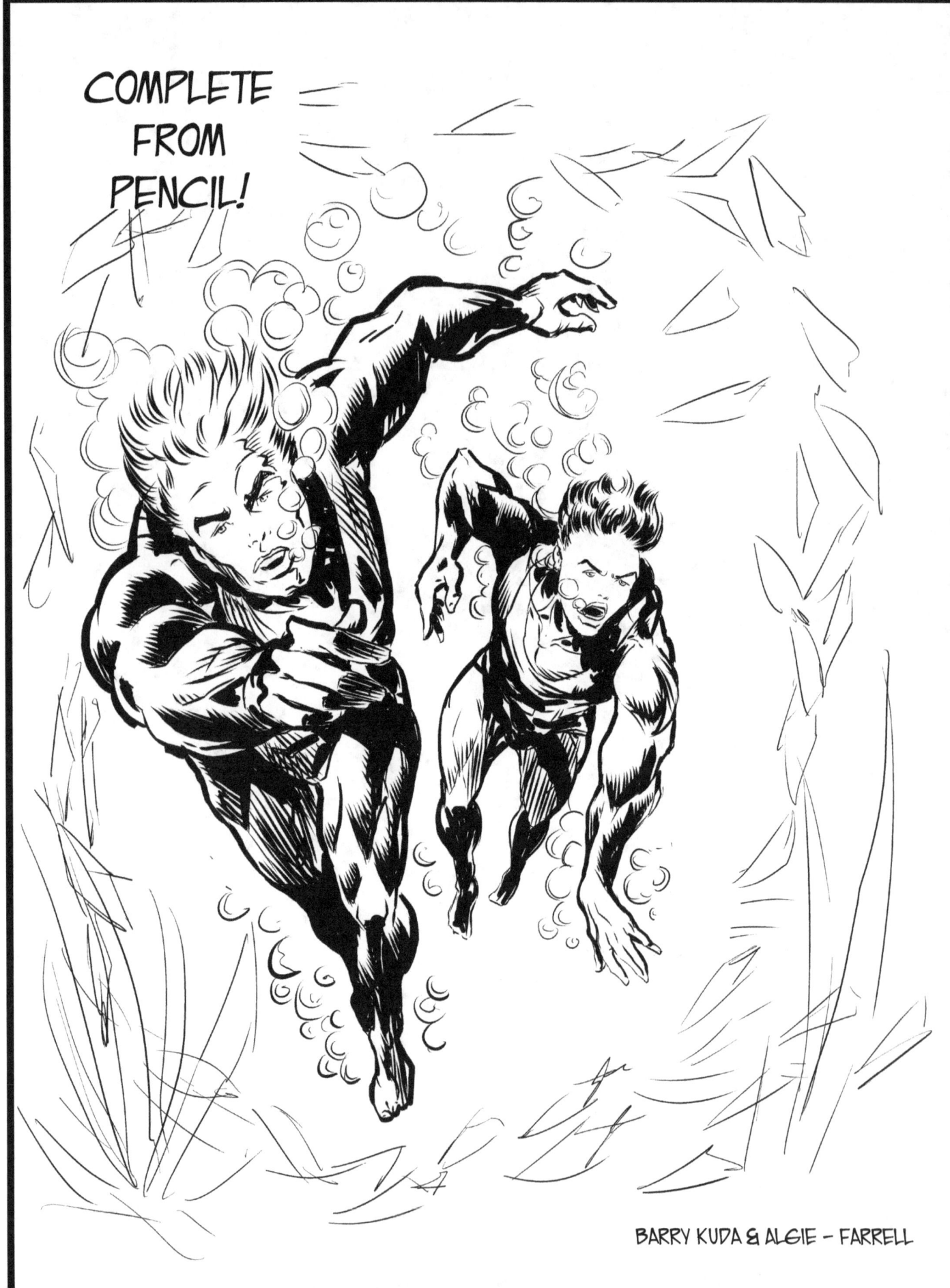

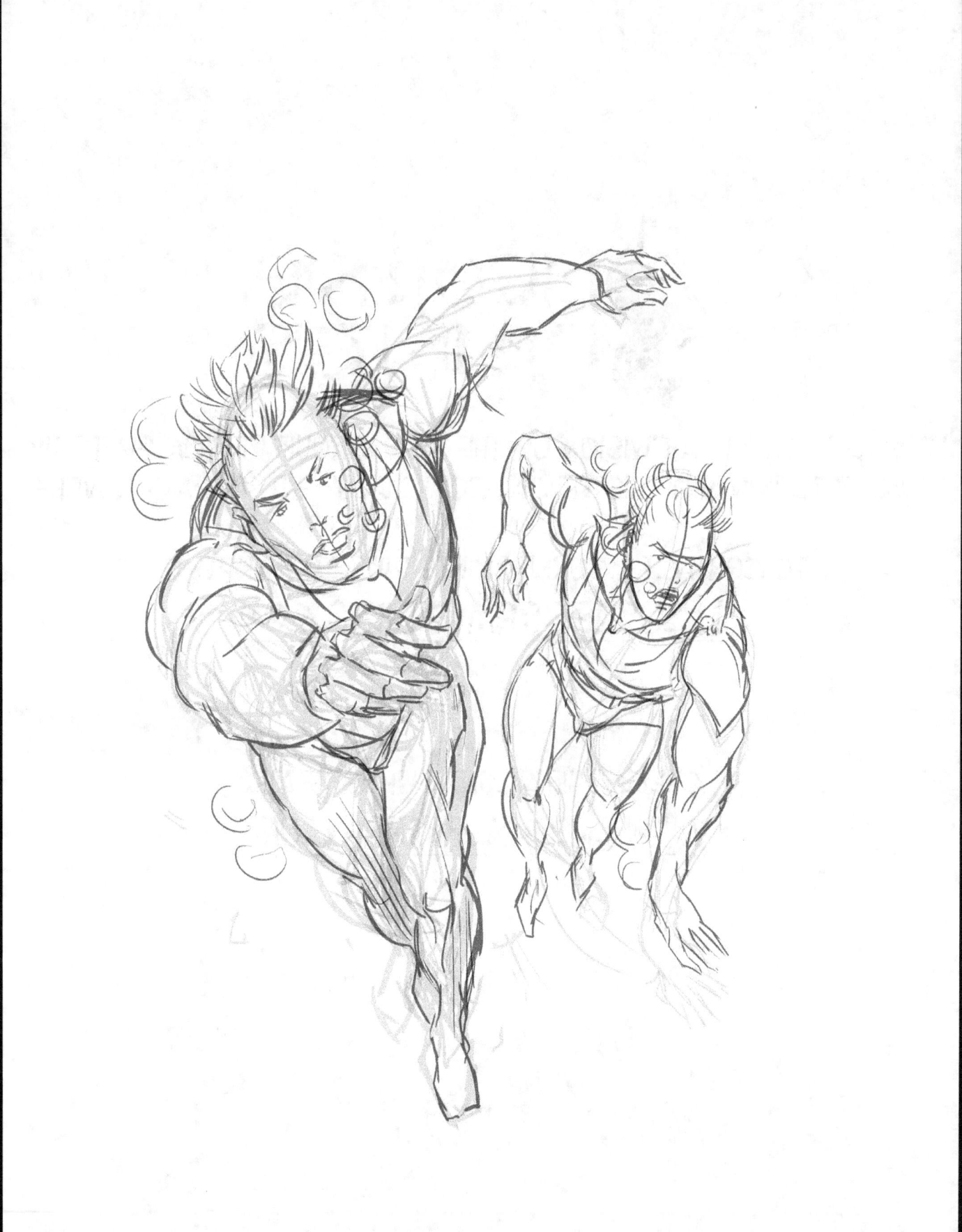

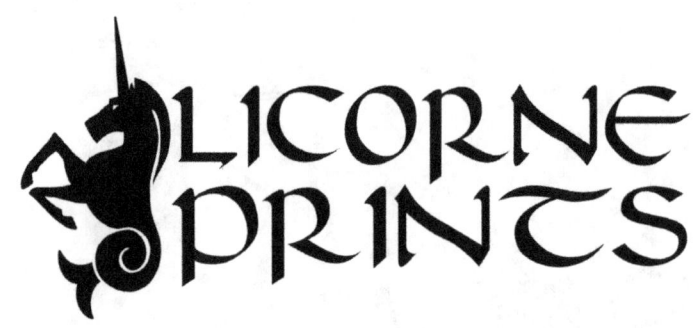

LICORNE PRINTS IS A DIVISION OF THE BMS GROUP DEDICATED TO HIGH QUALITY REPRINTS OF HISTORICAL COMIC BOOK STORIES AND NOVELS.

TO CONTACT LICORNE PRINTS DIRECTLY WRITE AT:
LICORNE@BEMYSTUDIO.COM

OR

CHECK THE LICORNE WEBSITE AT:
WWW.LICORNEPRINTS.COM

www.ingramcontent.com/pod-product-compliance
Lightning Source LLC
Chambersburg PA
CBHW081450220526
45466CB00008B/2584